Rave Re'

Within the drama of daily life, Wiggins and Wiggins effectively renders the process of writing and producing a play in Elizabethan England. This is an extraordinary lesson in Renaissance Theatre and Renaissance life. This novel makes me want to sit down to dinner with Good Will and have a serious talk about love and life.

Joy Gaines-Friedler,
Award-Winning Poet, Farmington Hills, MI

This book is written in a style easy to digest. It puts Will on a human scale as a person whose life was full of the trials and tribulations any of us might encounter. The difference here is that while he is endeavoring to keep his and his family's life on track, he is producing what will become world renowned literary works. The heart of this book, I believe, is to portray brilliance in human form as though he were your friend, relative, or neighbor.

Allen Galin,
Roving book critic, Scottsdale AZ

Outstanding "family dynamics!" Dialogue <u>very</u> convincing. Just a great read!! It's dramatic and has a feel of "authority" about it.

Paul D. Winston,
Retired Professor, Ann Arbor MI

For Nancy & Sam,

Good Will:
Shakespeare's Novel Life

Arthur W. Wiggins and Barbara M. Wiggins

*All the world's
a stage...!
(and we've been a
fair amount of
the players)
~ as you like it*

♡ Barbara & Art

First Edition Design Publishing
Sarasota, Florida USA

Good Will: Shakespeare's Novel Life
Copyright ©2019 Arthur W. Wiggins and Barbara M. Wiggins

ISBN 978-1506-908-44-1 AMZ PBK
ISBN 978-1506-908-43-4 TRADE PBK
ISBN 978-1506-908-45-8 EBK

LCCN 2019911528

August 2019

Published and Distributed by
First Edition Design Publishing, Inc.
P.O. Box 17646, Sarasota, FL 34276-3217
www.firsteditiondesignpublishing.com

*For those many
Shakespeare admirers
we met on our long
journey, those we
didn't meet and those
who have yet to
discover Good Will.
Enjoy.*

Prologue

I didn't write this novel. I write plays and poems.

In fact, I have written nothing the four hundred years since I shuffled off this mortal coil

But my plays have been presented and adapted into many languages and many lands. That thrills me. Some are better than others, but I applaud the creativity in these attempts, comparable to my efforts all those years ago. However, some things disturb me. Please indulge me pointing them out to you.

Generations of young people have been forced to read my plays as if they were literature. This is wrong. Words delivered on stage have emphasis, timbre, intonation and body language that is utterly absent from the word when it is merely written. Dry reading sucks the soul out of a living work. Read my plays if you must, but say the words aloud, even if you get funny looks. Better still, attend a theater performance so you can get the live flavor. Even videos or movies rank above tedious reading.

Next, fuzzy academics have searched records, dissected plays, run computer programs, and perhaps read tea leaves or crystals, searching for my real meanings in some kind of subtext or code. A few nitwits have even suggested it wasn't really me that wrote my plays. Well, I did have lots of assistance from other storytellers, players, and audiences. But the good lines and the bad ones are my responsibility. You'll see that from the story that follows

Finally, some people have written biographies, both factual and fictional about me. I suppose I should be flattered, but I saw no point of writing an autobiography because I doubted much of anyone would be interested. However, since you're reading this, I guess that makes you one of those few.

Now that you're prepared, feel free to dig into the rest of this novel. Some of it is accurate, some a little off. But you can judge for yourself if I am worthy of the title Good Will.

William Shakspeare

Chapter 1

Stratford

Spring 1582

> "Sweet are the uses of adversity
> Which, like the toad, ugly and venomous,
> Wears yet a precious jewel in his head."
> *As You Like It*

"Fire, fire!" yelled the town crier as he rang his bell.

Will looked up from his sewing and the needle punctured his finger, making him bleed all over the worktable. "Damn this wretched sewing." He dropped the glove he was stitching and wrapped his bleeding finger with the edge of a dye rag. "I should go see . . ."

Father slammed his hand on the wooden table. "What you need to do is to finish those gloves."

"But the fire might be Hamnet's bakery."

"Let the fire brigade do their job and you do yours."

"I can't just sit here if Hamnet is in trouble." Will headed toward the door.

Gilbert said, "I'll do his sewing tonight."

"You find any excuse to keep from working, Will Shakespeare. Don't you dare leave."

"Leave me alone. Gilbert is better anyway." Will stomped out and banged the door hard against the jamb, knocking it ajar. A wispy smoke column arose to Will's right. Not much of a fire, Will thought, and certainly not coming from the direction of the bakery. But he had no intention of turning around. Will set off toward the dense woods that served as his refuge whenever Father raged at him for his failures.

Gilbert ran after him, but Will turned and yelled at him to go back, "Maybe you can calm Father. He likes you better anyway."

The Shakespeare brothers were both teenagers, but Will was two years older, slightly heavier, and the recipient of far greater expectations. They were handsome lads, a little on the tall side, with brown hair and eyes. Father did like Gilbert better, probably because Will had an independent streak that Gilbert lacked. The parents often joked that Gilbert was his mother's son, while Will had more Shakespeare in him. Clashes between Will and Father had become more frequent as Will grew older, but they were like fireworks that flashed, then subsided quickly.

In the forest, the leaves were beginning their spring change, using the sun's energy to grow bigger and stronger. The sunny, mild day was treated to a slight breeze that promised warmer weather to come. Ordinarily, these surroundings might have calmed Will, but today he was too inwardly focused. Could Father be right? Was he just a bumbler who couldn't sew a glove, or accomplish anything worthwhile? Or was it just that more was expected of him as the eldest male? At a fork in the well-worn path, he took the less traveled branch towards the creek. He needed to be alone.

The clearing next to the creek came into view before he heard a women singing softly. She was in the water, stark naked, her long brown hair loose down her back and over her slim shoulders. He took a step forward, snapping a buried twig. She turned and shrieked. "Go away!"

"I . . .I . . .I . . . was just walking through the woods, minding my own business. I have as much right to this clearing as you have to that creek."

"Well, at least turn away while I get dressed!"

Will did as she said, but averted his gaze only slightly.

Just then, Gilbert burst into the clearing. "What have we here?"

"All accidental, I assure you." Will said.

"Both of you keep your eyes away from me!"

Gilbert laughed. "Looks like I'm unnecessary here. I'll head back to Henley Street. Father will be calmer by now." He beat a hasty retreat.

The young lady quickly pulled her dress over her slim body. She had left her undergarments and apron at home knowing she would bathe in the creek. "You are the first man to ever see me so exposed. I guess I should at least tell you my name. Anne Hathaway."

"I'm Will Shakespeare, the glover's son." Will bowed deeply. "I don't remember you at all."

"I'm stuck at home most of the time caring for my crabby step-mother."

"I don't know why she would be crabby with you around. Perhaps she's envious of your beauty. Now that you're dressed and we're introduced, I wonder if we might meet again under less stressful circumstances?"

"You could call on me at my house, Hewland Farm. My step-mother won't fault you if you do everything properly and you seem to know how to do that." Anne laughed. "I must be off to my chores."

Will smiled, waved, and turned back toward the woods, humming a little tune. Funny how a brief encounter with a person can change one's mood. Anne hath quite a way, he thought. Now he had even more to sort out.

Chapter 2

Temple Grafton

November 28, 1582

> "Excellent wretch!
> Perdition catch my soul But I do love thee!
> and when I love thee not, Chaos is come again."
> *Othello*

The wedding procession left Hewland Farm early Sunday morning. Though such processions were often raucous events, with gaiety, laughter, musicians, and song, this one was small and rather subdued. Besides the bride and groom, all others were family members of the Shakespeare and Hathaway clans, seventeen in all. Bound for St. Andrew's church in Temple Grafton, they enjoyed their hour-long journey along the dirt road on this clear, crisp autumn day.

"Why are we all they way out here, so far from home?" asked Gilbert.

"Blame it on the girl's father," said Father. "Although he died last year, his close friends promised they would look after his daughter when she married, and this is their home church." Besides that, he thought, they even posted a bond with the Bishop so that the marriage could take place after only one reading of the banns, and before Advent started.

Mother struggled to keep pace while carrying two-year old Edmund. She gazed at Will leading the parade. "What a fine man our eldest has grown to be. Look how handsome he looks in his new doublet and hose.

He's just tall enough, and he has my Arden high forehead. Full of brains, I'm sure."

Father thought, he does look good, but now that he's married, he can't complete his apprenticeship to enter any profession. "Gilbert, I hope you'll never fall for some woman before you are earning a good living. Will has not set a good example to you and your brothers."

"Now, Father, don't forget Anne's dowry from her father's will," said Mother.

"Don't you forget the gloves I made as wedding presents for her whole family. I'm sure Will will pay us some of that, but with more mouths to feed, it won't last long, the way my business is going." Father was thankful they were away from Stratford where few, if any, of his clients would see the procession.

Richard, who was just eight, ran around Joan, age eleven, poking her in the side. Anne's younger siblings matched their energy and distraction – she also had a brother Richard. They all ran rings around the grown-ups.

On the other side of the procession, Anne's younger brother Bartholomew walked with his wife, Isabella. She walked with some effort, as she was quite large with her first pregnancy. She had been married only a year and suspected Anne was with child. "Anne's clothes are quite colorful, and the herb bouquet she carries is lovely. Too bad it's too late in the year for nice flowers."

"Yes, yes. Anne is quite splendid." Too bad her dowry is lost to us, Bartholomew thought. We could use it at the estate. We could also use her help with mother. My poor wife will have both a new baby and an aging mother-in-law to care for, along with all my other siblings.

Joan Hathaway, Anne's step-mother, worried that she would not be able to cope without Anne's help. Isabella would not be up to the task with her first-born added to the household. They would have to hire one of the neighbor girls, which would only add to their money woes.

Will looked over the marching group and thought about how life can change in the strangest ways from one chance meeting. He wondered if everyone had similar experiences. Then he said to Anne: "How happy the families look together. This is a good sign for our marriage." Anne smiled up at him, hoping he was right. Then she squeezed his hand.

Soon, the procession arrived at St. Andrews, an old church too large for its congregation, a reminder of a bygone era for the now small village. They were met at the church door by the pastor, who welcomed them and blessed the plain gold family ring Will had brought for Anne. The group then entered the church and stood as the service progressed. At the end, the pastor blessed the couple again, and they pronounced the classic marriage vows. Will smiled and said:

"I, William, take you, Anne, to be my wife, to have and to hold from this day forward, for better or for worse, for richer, for poorer, in sickness and in health, to love and to cherish, until death do us part."

In turn, Anne quietly spoke her part, and the bride and groom kissed. Soon, a new Shakespeare would join them.

Chapter 3

Stratford

1585

"Let him fear this, for it will come to pass
that every braggart shall be found an ass."
All's Well that Ends Well

Six months later, Susanna Shakespeare was born, and little more than two years after that, another celebration centered on Will and Anne: the birth of twins, Hamnet and Judith.

For three straight days, Mother had worked without rest to make sure everyone was fed and the house kept tidy. She was always on the move and retained her girlish figure and long auburn hair. Even Father set to work building a second cradle without complaint. The morning of the christening, Father shocked everyone by offering to keep Richard home with him during the church service at Holy Trinity.

Mother carried baby Hamnet on the way to church, while Anne carried his sister Judith as they walked briskly to keep warm against the winter wind. They were a hardy bunch, but only Hamnet carried the Shakespeare name to the next generation.

Will walked with Susanna who toddled along and babbled about everything and nothing at the same time. With her bouncing blond curls and sweet chatter, she charmed everyone.

When they arrived at the church, Judith Sadler beamed at Anne, and took her thin arm. Judith Sadler was a bit chubby, and always ready to lend a helping hand. "You and baby Judith come right in with me and sit down before you faint." Judith's husband Hamnet Sadler was an undersized, powerfully built fellow who was short on hair, but long on humor. He immediately launched into a story about a baker who put one loaf of bread into the oven, but when he pulled it out, it had split in two. He made a lot more money by selling each loaf as a miracle.

Mary Shakespeare and her grandson Hamnet relaxed in the front pew for a moment while the others got settled. She leaned forward to gaze at the family Will had brought into their home. It had been almost as cold as today that April, almost twenty one years ago, when she sat in the same pew with the infant Will. She recalled that long frigid winter when countless families shrank as the plague struck down relative after relative. The birth of a baby was a great blessing, but it also brought a great fear.

Harkening back to those years ago, in her reverie state, Mary remembered her sister Alice's tart words, "Your William sleeps quietly right now, but I pray he doesn't cry the whole time like your other two did." Alice was one of her older sisters, and had a very prim demeanor to go with her thinness.

Mary never understood how Alice could say such an unkind thing about her babies in heaven. Both girls were sick and couldn't help crying. Then came the rest of Alice's complaint: "I walked a long way for this service. I came because it is the respectable thing to do, not because I have any desire to witness the christening of another nephew. Afterwards, I must hurry home and continue my chores. I have no husband or children to help, only a mother who cannot do for herself."

"I know it's not easy for you, Alice. Thank you for coming, you make our family complete.

But then, Alice softened, and gazed at baby Will again. "I must confess your son seems content enough this day. He awakens, yet remains peaceful in spite of his disagreeable aunt."

"I am blessed with a healthy baby and a dear husband who says extra prayers for him. You know, Alice, my John is a hard worker, and our children love him just like we loved our father. Remember when all eight of us girls scrambled to sit on his lap after supper, when he settled in his big oak chair by the fire and told stories of his childhood?"

"Aye, and you got more than your share, being the youngest."

"No, not the way I remember it."

"Yes, "tis, so don't argue. I still remember him telling us tales of our ancestors. I can still quote him, 'Your great-great grandfather Arden lost all our land to William the Conqueror in the great bloody battle of Wickinsham. He suffered terrible hardship but our family never gave up. We just kept working, year after year, to get our land back. Even those who had no sons, as we have none. By grandfather's time, we regained all our lost land, and more. Park Hall, where your cousins live now, is part of that very soil. Girls, never you forget, whoever you marry, you are an Arden, and your sons will have strong Arden blood in their veins.'"

Mary laughed at Alice's mimicry, thinking: "I hope father was right. I named our first born son after the family home at Wilmcote, hoping the name would forge a link with the Ardens. Perhaps he will become the son father never had."

Before she sat down, Alice quietly reached over and ran the side of her little finger across Will's smooth pink cheek. "Your mother has high hopes for you, little lad. I pray you please her." Then, abruptly, Alice pulled back her hand and said, "It's not my lot in life to have such blessings of God as you and our sisters. I have Mother instead. May God grant your son and my other nephews the grace and strength to carry on our family traditions."

Mary looked up with a start. She was holding Hamnet, and Will was speaking to her. "Mother, Mother, it's time for me to take Hamnet up to the christening font."

"Oh, yes. I must have been lost in prayer." She handed the sleeping Hamnet to his father, repeating a prayer similar to the one Alice prayed almost twenty one years ago.

After the church ceremony, family and friends gathered at the Shakespeare home, which was decorated with dried flowers and herbs and filled with celebrating friends and family. Everyone admired the fine feast of breads, fish, carrots, onions, radishes and cheese that was set out on the large dining table. There was just enough room for everyone to move about the large area that Father created when he joined the two Henley Street houses.

"I raise my cup to all family and friends. Let us celebrate the baptism of Hamnet and Judith. May their purity guide them to live long and happy lives," Will said. The assembled crowd drank the toast with good cheer.

Hamnet Sadler went over to Will. "Judith and I are so honored that you chose us for god-parents. We will do everything in our power to make sure your children lead worthy lives."

"I hope you remember that when they come to your bakery for treats," said Will. "Look, Susanna isn't even two yet, and she's already going after the teething biscuits." Indeed, Susanna had tottered over to the sweets table and grabbed a treat. "Joan, please get her." Will asked his sister. He felt the warmth of pride as he looked over his family.

When the party thinned out, Father pulled Will into the workshop to speak to him. "The celebration and sentiments are wonderful, but costly. Living with eleven people in this house creates a huge strain that will only increase as these babies grow. We don't even have any spare rooms for tenants, as before."

"Like those last renters? They only paid half the time anyway before they slipped away in the middle of the night," said Will.

"Eleven mouths to feed is no small task, Will. I'm sorely pressed." Father turned red in the face.

"Calm yourself. Affairs will change; they always do."

"Calm? The glove business has fallen off, and nobody wants to buy my wool. You need to contribute more, instead of putting your nose in a book or writing nonsense with your friends."

Will laughed. "Business doesn't control our whole lives. How about letting nature provide? My friends and I won't just write about the woods, we'll harvest game from them, and fill our tables."

"With three children of your own now, you need to start hunting more than wild animals." Father shook his head and walked away.

Charlecote was a lovely estate, perhaps the finest for miles around. The grounds covered 185 acres on the River Avon and the large manor house had been rebuilt in 1558 in red brick. The current lord of the manor was Sir Thomas Lucy, a tall, slender, almost effeminate man with reddish hair and beard. He served as local magistrate for the area, and represented Warwickshire in Parliament. Today, Sir Thomas was seated at a large desk in the manor house, frowning at the two men before him, Father and Will Shakespeare. Several Lucy servants stood nearby.

"Young man, my game wardens tell me they caught you red-handed with the carcass of a deer. What do you have to say for yourself?"

"Indeed, that's true, sir. But there is no law against hunting deer outside a park, is there?"

"Don't presume to tell me about law. The problem isn't about any deer park. You were trespassing on my property."

"The deer had been wounded some distance off, and we were just tracking her."

"How convenient. You shall receive twenty lashes to sharpen your powers of boundary observation."

Will wasn't surprised; he had expected this punishment or worse.

"And you, Shakespeare the elder. I've heard rumors about you loaning money and collecting interest. The law is very clear on this matter: 'Usury is a vice most odious and detestable.' Stiff fines and imprisonment await those who collect usurious interest. What say you?"

"Pure fabrication, your lordship. Competitors are jealous of my service on the town council and make trouble for me with their lies."

"Since there is rumor but no proof, no action will be taken, but you are hereby warned. There is another thing, not a rumor, but a fact. Your wife is from the Arden family, and there were Ardens involved in a Catholic plot against our great Queen Elizabeth. What knowledge of any plots do you or your wife have?"

"We did hear of some distant relatives in difficulty, but my wife and her family are steadfastly loyal to Queen Elizabeth and the Church of England. You can be assured of that. There is no doubt."

"But your church attendance is spotty of late. Might that be an indicator of disloyalty?"

"Not at all, your Lordship. My family is quite large, and child problems have made us stay home rather than be a distraction to the rest of the congregation."

"Children need to go to church so they can be raised well. See that you are more diligent about church attendance. One more thing. What do you know about this scurrilous trash?" Lucy handed a piece of parchment to one of his servants, who showed it to Father and Will.

A parliemente member, a justice of peace,
At home a poor scare-crowe, at London an asse,
If lowsie is Lucy, as some volke miscalle it,
Then Lucy is lowsie whatever befall it.
He thinks himself greate,Yet and asse in his state,
We allowe by his ears but with asses to mate.

Lucy glared at Will. "Young man, do you know something about this libelous poem?"

"No, sir. I've never seen it before. It doesn't even rhyme well."

"What is this country coming to? Plots against the Queen, Catholics creating disorder, money-lenders charging interest, scurrilous writing defaming a person's good name. I even heard that some vagabond players, not content to stay in the evil London, tour the countryside to fleece ordinary people and take their money to watch immoral plays. There is even a troupe of them on their way to Stratford right now. Is that some of your town council's doing?"

"I no longer serve on the council, but I know they do license entertainment from time to time. The people enjoy it."

Sir Thomas Lucy gave a deep sigh and buried his head in his hands for a moment, then looked directly at Father and Will. "Entertainment? It's evil stories." He turned to his servants, "Give this young man his lashes and send them both on their way." He then addressed both Father and Will: "If you create any more trouble, I'll find out, and you will learn what real trouble is. Get them out of my sight."

The lashes were administered none too gently. Will gritted his teeth and held his breath. It was worth it, he thought, even as he bled. When it was over, Father helped Will stand up and silently led him on the two mile walk home, where Mother would place healing compresses on his wounds. A distant rainstorm treated them to occasional flashes of lightning and the rumble of thunder.

As they walked, Father said, "That poem. I hope you didn't write it."

"Not exactly. Hamnet Sadler had a run-in with one of Lucy's men who was almost as arrogant as his master. I helped Hamnet a little, but he writes pretty well for a baker, don't you think?"

"Oh, Will . . ."

"Father, I know your concern for mother's Arden relatives, and I'm sure she would have been proud of the way you defended them. But what was that about money-lending?"

"That is not your concern. Right now, everybody's business is bad, and rumors and lies travel quickly. With Lucy watching me like a hawk, I'll have to lay low. We're in a quandary here."

"Father, don't worry. I'll cause no more trouble with Lucy. If you can just take care of Anne and the children for a while, I'll have to vanish and find some other place to make money. Lucy may be lousy, but I got an idea from some of his blather. I must try something different."

Chapter 4

London

Summer 1589

> "And since you know you cannot see yourself,
> so well as by reflection, I, your glass,
> will modestly discover to yourself,
> that of yourself which you yet know not of."
>
> *Julius Caesar*

Sir Thomas Lucy's prediction about a traveling troupe of players proved quite accurate, and they left Stratford with one more member – Will. Although he knew nothing about plays, he was a quick study, and contributed his store of knowledge about the countryside and a good amount of manual labor to the troupe. The tour ended in London, and the good news was that the tour's leader, James Burbage, had taken a liking to Will and asked him to stay on with the troupe when they performed. The bad news was that his pay was barely above starvation level. Sometimes Will missed Stratford's quiet slow pace as much as he missed his family. However, as time moved along, Will learned quite a lot about plays and how to navigate the crowded, noisy, smelly streets of London.

St. Paul's Cathedral stood guard over the jam-packed plaza. Everyone from the Lord Mayor to the filthiest thief went there, not only to worship and make social contacts but to conduct business. Will often walked amongst the crowds because he always saw something that amazed him. He regarded a visit to St. Paul's as one of the prime entertainments in London. On this hot and humid day, the Cathedral's bulk cast a welcome cooling shadow on the bookstalls that lined the entrance where Will intended to meet Richard Field.

Without warning, a solidly-built fellow dressed all in black stepped out of the crowd and grabbed Will's arm. He twisted it behind Will's back and hissed into his ear, "You've been avoiding me. Where's my money?"

"Don't worry. You'll get it, I promise."

"Promises are cheap. You need to give me real money soon, or you'll regret it the rest of your life." The fellow's foul breath made Will wince, and the pressure increased.

"You'll get nothing if I cannot use that arm to write a play."

The pressure relaxed only slightly. "A play? Those don't always make money, you know."

"James Burbage will pay me regardless. You'll get your money. I just need more time."

"Well, the Burbages are better with money than what I hear about Shakespeares. But, if I have to come looking for you again, you'll have to write that drivel with broke fingers." The black-clad fellow released Will's arm and moved into the shadows as quickly as he had appeared.

Will shuddered and rubbed his arm as he moved toward the booksellers.

He scanned the crowd for Richard's face when he heard a horse's hoofs on the stone path behind him. He jumped aside as the horse and rider raced past him, directly into St. Paul's as if it were an open road. People inside simply stepped away to allow passage.

Then Will spotted Richard Field. "Did you see that horse go right through St. Paul's?"

Richard Field laughed, "Sure. If the shortest way goes straight through, then that's how they go. There might be some law against it, but city folks live by a different set of manners."

"So I'm learning. Walking London's streets is an education unlike any I've known. As is Holinshed's *Chronicles*, the book you just lent me. How else would I learn all the histories about England, Scotland, and

Ireland? If our schoolmaster in Stratford had these, he might have added a lot to our studies."

"I only loan books to you because of your long friendship with my brother back home. In London, only private tutors teach history and Holinshed is something I can sell a lot of."

Will looked at the pile of books Richard had set out. "How long must you stay here? Perhaps you could loan me another history book or we could share a meal."

"I'm stuck here all day. Another time . . . but stay a moment, I see someone who will amuse us both." Richard shouted over the din. "Kit, Kit Marlowe. Over here."

A slightly-built figure with a black cloak and a tall hat turned and surveyed the sour-smelling, noisy crowd until he caught sight of Richard. He smiled in recognition, tilted his hat and ambled toward the bookstall.

He placed a multi-ringed hand on each of Richard's shoulders and kissed both cheeks. "Greetings, Richard. What news from the publishing world?"

"Little new, but you know Vaultrollier's always publishes the best."

"You wish." Kit glanced at Will. "Who's your friend, some new book seller?"

"I am William Shakespeare. Are you the Marlowe who wrote *Tamburlaine the Great?*"

"Indeed. And were you one of the groundlings at an Admiral's Men performance of my play?"

"Oh, yes. The magnificent language soared above any play I had ever seen."

"A groundling who understood the words? Hard to fathom."

Richard Field said, "Will is more than a groundling. He works for James Burbage with Lord Strange's Men."

Kit eyed Will up and down. "So, one of Burbage's boys, eh? He pays way more poorly than Henslowe at the Admiral's Men, no wonder you look like a book seller. What do you do for him, pray tell?"

"Anything James Burbage wants. Most recently, he's set me to mending lines in poorly-written plays."

"You look about my age, and sturdy too. I didn't see you at Cambridge; did you attend Oxford?"

"No, I came up the hard way. I joined a traveling troupe in Stratford and stayed with them all winter and back to London."

"Ha. This town eats up and spits out people like you. Perhaps you'll see another of my plays, Shakeman, before you return to your humble roots in the country. Well, I must be off to more important matters." Kit waved airily and sauntered off.

Richard Field turned to Will. "I hope he didn't insult you too badly. He can be quite offensive."

"So I see. Richard, please do me a favor. Show me anything Kit Marlowe writes, anything."

"Certainly, Will. I usually don't get plays, but I'll keep an eye out for his. Jacqueline and I would be pleased if you would join us for supper some evening. You might enjoy being back in the chaos of children."

"That's very appealing, but until then, I must work with diligence to keep Marlowe's prediction from becoming reality."

Chapter 5

London

Summer 1590

"I drink to the general joy o' the whole table."
Macbeth

In his rented room above a tavern, Will woke up and stretched his arms behind him. His wrist ached. Then he saw the line of sunlight that ran across the floor. He was late. The foolscap lay on the table in front of him. A black stain marked the place where he had fallen asleep with pen still in hand. He reached for the dried-up ink bottle and threw it at the wall. More waste.

Will sprinted up Shoreditch, barely avoiding collisions with people going about their morning business-- meeting people, sweeping the street, carrying out the evening waste, getting water from the nearest well, hurrying children along and the ever-present pick-pockets. James Burbage waited at The Theatre for Will to deliver the manuscript of a play about Henry VI. After the defeat of the Spanish Armada last year, James took the chance that play-going audiences would enjoy history plays. James had such a play already written by Kit Marlowe, but didn't like it, and couldn't work with Marlowe, so he took a chance on Will. When the black timbers of The Rose became visible, Will broke into a final run. His breathing was labored by the time he stood on the edge of the stage across from the short and stout Richard Burbage. Although several years younger than Will, he was the owner's son and had the privilege and experience to go with it.

"Did you run all the way here?" Richard raised a gleaming, unsheathed sword to dueling position.

"Who are you dueling, a ghost?" Will said.

"I'm dueling you, my friend, no matter what you have in hand."

"And what is the cause of our duel if I'm your friend?"

"I need practice for the performance today lest I offend the great Ned Alleyn. And it's punishment for your being late." Richard faked a lunge at Will. "Not to mention that in another play, you almost removed my wig with one of your awkward thrusts. This is not a comedy." He lowered his sword.

"The angle of your wig goes with your sharp tongue," Will said.

"Get your dull sword and be quick about it. Don't even bother to attire yourself in the tiring house."

Will found a short knife under a pile of costumes in the tiring house and took a sword that hung on the wall. On stage, both held long swords in their right hands and daggers in their left. Richard started to parry.

"You need to relax and think about not allowing me to kill you," Richard said. "Move back when I lunge, set yourself up for a move toward me. Pretend I'll take away your favorite bed partner if I win."

Will laughed and moved to parry. "You're distracted by thoughts of the fairer sex." He lunged. "You're in trouble."

Richard sidestepped neatly. "Speaking of trouble, when Father arrives, he'll want to see the changes you made to that Marlowe play."

"Not your worry," Will said. Beads of sweat formed on his brow. Back and forth they went. The dull sound of their boots on the wooden floor made a harmonious counterpoint to the zing of steel against steel from their swords.

"Enough, villains." Ned Alleyn strode onto the stage, took off his cape and handed it off to one of the young boys from the troupe. His large size and powerful physique always commanded attention. "Make way for someone who knows what they're doing. Put those swords away and be off with you both!" He moved to stage center and stretched like a cat after a long nap.

Will bowed to Ned and left with Richard. "Off with your tongue, vile bastard," he said, under his breath.

"Last night someone threw a rotten pear at him."

"They should have thrown a whole orchard."

"Shakespeare," James yelled from the tiring house. His voice boomed louder than normal from this normally handsome and charming fellow. "Have you finally fixed that Henry play?" He ran down the stage steps.

"It's inside my tunic, safe from Richard's sword and ready for the Master of the Revels," Will said.

"For months you've been working on this. It had best be as good as *Tamburlaine*." James grabbed the tied-up sheets of foolscap and scanned them. "It's even more poetic and intricate than Marlowe. I'm not sure the players can handle it, especially Ned Alleyn." James shook the foolscap in Will's face. "I've no more time to waste. If Master of the Revels Tilney approves, we'll have to try it." He re-tied the bundle. "I'm not paying you unless the box office takings are good."

Hours later, James returned. "Tilney was quick about it for me. He wants a few changes to appease the Queen. Now fix them and be just as quick."

Will grabbed the foolscap from James and read through the black marks. "That pernicious bloodsucker of sleeping men will be the ruin of me. How can I worry about the Queen's feelings and write lines the players can handle, and audience will like? Find someone to play my part in today's performance. I have to buy ink and candles. And I need money."

"I'll give you three pence and expect you back at first light tomorrow," James said. "Now move."

The following day, Will handed James the revised play. "I stayed up all night, and pray my efforts be judged fairly."

James laughed. "The real judgment comes when the audience hears your lines. While I see Tilney, you can work on those props."

"Don't expect me to stay up another night," Will yelled at James's stooped back.

Will wandered into the tiring house and found Richard pulling out old props from an overflowing wooden trunk. "Let's go to The George for supper. I need to celebrate finishing that play mending."

"What part is mine?"

"You should be King Henry and Ned should be making his grand gestures on someone else's stage."

"Not likely. I tried to tell Father."

"And he said. . . ?"

"The same as he always says about Ned marrying Henslowe's daughter and the profits we might lose if he leaves."

"Oh, to be the prophet of profits. I need a plan to make that dunghill of a knave disappear so you can use my words to take center stage."

"You've concocted an idea?"

"One swims about in my head," Will said.

"You know that handkerchief Ned always waves about?"

"He brags it's from his betrothed."

"Could it show up elsewhere?" Will asked.

"How?"

"I haven't formed the whole scene. Suppose he drank too much and..."

"And Henslowe's daughter would find him in bed with a wench? Too good to happen," said Richard. "Back to the handkerchief."

"Maybe we could combine both ideas."

"Now we have two things to celebrate. Let's go."

The George was a popular, noisy pub that was part of an inn, making it dark and full of entertaining opportunities. Patrons sat with friends on hard, wooden benches pulled up to heavy, long tables. Moll, who always sought out her favorite players, met them at their usual table, set in a corner where they could practice lines if need be. Moll's long dark hair made her pleasant-looking, but her lace bodice strained to keep her flesh in, and she was no longer young. "I'd say good day, but you two look like nothing's good. Have yourself some ale."

"Tell me Moll, what do the serving girls think of Ned Alleyn?" Will asked.

"Ha. He never leaves us no extra. Says it's enough privilege just to serve him."

Will looked around. "Will you help us play a little trick on him?"

"You can count on me. Now give me your order before we get too busy."

Will looked at Richard. "It may cost you a few pence, but you could end up with the role of the King."

"Tell me more."

That night at The George, everyone was gathered for the laughter, food and drinking. Even Ned ignored the teasing of his fellow players, while he downed free ale Moll claimed was from a secret admirer. After many rounds, the innkeeper whispered in Ned's ear.

Ned stood up. "A devotee of my superior acting talents requests a private word with me and I must accommodate my fans." He strode grandly up the stairs. Moll whispered to another barmaid, "Cover for me a bit, love." And followed Ned with a full pitcher of ale.

Soon after, a young barmaid went upstairs and Moll returned with the well-known handkerchief stuffed in her bosom. She stood next to their table checking to see if any of the players needed something to drink.

"Say, how did you come by that pretty handkerchief, Moll?" Henry Condell asked.

"Just never you mind." Moll fluttered her eyelashes.

Ned Alleyn did not reappear that night.

The next day, scribes finished Henry VI, Part 2 and James announced the whole company was to meet at The George for supper and to assign parts. Will arrived late and had to crowd in with eight of his fellow actors at one of the long wooden table. They were in the back corner as usual, away from the noise of prostitutes, entertainers, hucksters and servants. Ned watched James shoulder his way in, holding a large bundle of rolled-up papers still smelling of the paste the scribes used to put the sheets together. He dumped them on the table to loud cheers. "You better remain cheerful through rehearsals, because this must be on stage in ten days."

"We'll have to rehearse every morning at first light," Will Kempe said.

"That's right. Henslowe has a new play out." James passed out the rolls and each player quickly read through his lines.

"What's this tangle of words?" Ned Alleyn yelled. "I can't use these lines. They are way too long and wordy."

"Try saying them instead of using them," Richard said.

"Someone should cut off your tongue," Ned said. "You and Shakespeare did this."

"Why not try speaking the words as they're written?" Will asked.

"Bah! Your words mean nothing. People come to see me, not to hear your fancy phrases."

"Why can't they have both?" Will asked.

"No country bumpkin will tell me what to do," Ned said. He handed his roll to Will. "Change my lines if you want me in this play."

"Anyone want to order now?" Moll stood at the end of the table with the handkerchief from the night before tucked in her bosom.

"Moll, go away. We have work to do," James said.

Ned stood and patted his pockets. "That's my handkerchief. How did you get it?"

"Since you don't remember, I guess it's for me to know and you to figure out," Moll said.

"It's mine." Ned reached for the handkerchief. "Give it to me."

Moll stepped back. "Maybe your admirer last night took it when you fell asleep."

"Another great performance, Ned?" Richard said.

James slammed his fist on the table. "Sit down, Ned. This is an important play and we need to rehearse to make it sound good."

"Isn't that the handkerchief your betrothed gave you?" Will asked.

Ned turned redder. "I never let that handkerchief out of my sight."

James walked over to Moll and grabbed the handkerchief. "Now sit down, all of you. We have work to do."

"Give it to me." Ned lunged.

James stepped back.

"That must be what your admirer said." Will Kempe shouted from the other end.

"I'll not be made a laughingstock by you." Ned pointed his finger at James.

"By me? Here, take your foolish prop." James tossed the handkerchief. As it floated down, two players grabbed it.

"Dance for it, Ned." Will Kempe jumped onto the table and did a quick jig.

"I won't dance for you scurvy fools." Ned grabbed the handkerchief. "You'll regret this when Henslowe and I take your audience. Richard, you're lucky you're the owner's son. And you, Shakespeare, you'll never be a player. You can't even mend plays." Ned stormed out.

"A pox on all of you." James slammed the table again with his fist. "Without Ned Alleyn, how will be attract an audience?"

"Without Ned Alleyn, our actors are better than Henslowe's," Will said.

"He's right," Henry Condell said. "Ned ruins it for the rest of us when he seizes the center of the stage and makes up the lines as he goes on at full volume."

"Who can handle the role of the King?" James shouted back.

"What about me?" Richard said.

"We can't take a chance on someone the audience doesn't know."

"Why not?" Henry Condell said. "I think they'll like Richard better."

Will stood. "I know what Richard can do; I wrote that part with him in mind. Richard will add to our troupe's reputation."

"Will you wager your pay on it?" James asked.

Will looked at Richard. "Double or nothing."

One week later, Will climbed the five stairs leading from the groundlings' dirt floor pit to the stage. He looked up at the scrub ladies cleaning the lord's rooms. One of them leaned over the rail and yelled to Will. "Say us some of them pretty words."

"Get yourself back to work," Cuthbert Burbage yelled from a lower seat behind the groundlings' pit. Cuthbert, Richard's brother, was two years older than Richard, but shorter and heavier and a lot more serious.

Will scanned the semi-circle of seats until he saw him. Cuthbert sounded like Father. He couldn't stand to see anyone take a break. Cuthbert walked toward Will.

"Since the cursed fog is burning off, a crowd will surely come to see our new play as long as the weather holds." Cuthbert looked toward the dark clouds in the sky.

"Hey Will, sit down and have a pear," Richard yelled from a bench in the lower gallery. "Let the sweet nectar calm you."

"It won't help." He couldn't believe that before a performance, Richard would lie down and eat fruit like a Roman emperor. "And you sound like a piglet at its sow's teat."

"I indulge myself before every performance."

"Then allow me my indulgence for some peace and quiet. I need to think through the changes and some of the staging."

"Where's Father?" Cuthbert said.

"In the tiring house." Richard got up and met Will. He bowed dramatically and removed an imaginary hat.

"Let me see now. . . my good playwright . . .
do I part with a penny to stand on my feet,
next to the stage, no place for a seat?
Or shall it be twopenny to sit in the boxes,
hoping to find myself some foxes.
Better yet, send the wench for a threepenny seat
and tell her to check that the cushion is neat."

"You mock me." Will frowned. "This is my first play. It means everything to me."

"You're too serious. If they don't like it, I'm the one who'll have to duck all the rotten pears."

"Richard, I speak of more than disgruntled groundlings."

"This *Henry* fits the history idea like *Tamburlaine*. We all like it. And if Father likes it, it must be good." Richard tossed the pear core to the side of the pit. "We can try bear baiting if the audience isn't pleased."

Will smiled. "I can bear no more of your idle chatter. I'm going back to the tiring house." Will went through the doorway at the back of the stage and almost ran into Henry Condell rushing by with his script in one hand and his costume in the other.

Two hours later, a long series of trumpet blasts announced the start and eleven players took their places on stage. Henry Condell, as the Duke of Suffolk, spoke the first words:

As by your high imperial majesty
I had in charge my depart for France,
As procurator to your excellence,
To marry Princess Margaret for your grace,

Will watched the actors' every move and the audience's reaction. The words fell into place allowing him to sit down behind the tiring house curtain. He stroked his new mustache. It felt good.

James sat next to him. "The crowd makes less noise than usual. Perhaps they're sleeping."

"Or listening," Will said. "It's time for me to go on."

Will went on stage to deliver a message to the King and when he finished, he looked down at the groundlings. They watched the players move about the stage; they were fascinated.

When the Duke of York wrested the crown from Henry VI, he announced:

Look in a glass, and call thy image so:
I am thy king, and thou a false-heart traitor.
Call hither to the stake my two brave bears,

Lord Clifford responded:

Are these thy bears? we'll bait thy bears to death, And manacle the bear-ward in their chains, If thou dare bring them to the baiting place.

Will laughed. "You know, we've actually got some of the bear audience and no one left early to go see them."

James' smile made his scruffy beard expand. "The bears would never have the nerve to mention us."

The Duke of Warwick proclaimed:

. . . 'twas a glorious day:
Saint Alban's battle won by famous York
Shall be eternized in all age to come
Sound drums and trumpets, and to London all;
And more such days as these to us befall!

The audience applauded, shouted, and stomped until the wood beneath Will's feet shook. They shouted for the players to come back on stage. Someone yelled, "What happens next?"

Richard took Will's arm. "Let's go out and take a bow," he yelled to the players in the tiring house.

They were thrilled and ran out half-dressed in their costumes, eager to hear the applause. Backstage, the players were pleased with the performance and told Will, one after another, how much they liked it. He'd never had such praise. Without the head start from Marlowe and Holinshed, he'd never be here, Will thought.

James came over and handed Will a bag of coins. "You were right about the audience loving the play."

Will smiled.

James said, "But Ned Alleyn was right about something, too. You're not a very good player. A play mender maybe, or even a playwright, but not a player. No big rolls for you."

Chapter 6

Stratford

1591

"The game is up."
Cymbeline

When Father built the rooms that joined the two adjacent houses on Henley Street, it made the kitchen into the largest room in the house. They needed the extra space with ten Shakespeares to feed and little ones to watch. Mother, Joan, and Anne Shakespeare stood at the table, cutting greens. Anne said to Mother: "So, I'm not the first Anne Shakespeare, am I?

"Not at all. My daughter Anne would have been twenty this year. I still feel saddened that she is not with us. You remember her, Joan."

"Oh, yes. I loved my little sister. She was so frail at the end."

Anne continued, "But, when I spoke to Father about her, he said something about a Shakespeare curse, gave me a dark look, and walked away."

"Since he turned sixty, Father has grown more superstitious than ever. There was a strange incident more than a decade ago, and it changed Father a lot. Now it seems to haunt him more. He acts like it just happened."

"It must have been something powerful."

"Oh, it was. Bishop Whitgrift had just been installed, and he came into town to preach a Christmas sermon and have the townspeople meet him. Father was town Bailiff, and he wanted to impress the new Bishop. But before we even entered the church, Anne started one of her coughing fits."

Joan said, "She couldn't stop. Her face turned red and it sounded like she was going to cough out her lungs."

"In order not to disrupt the service, Father picked her up and ducked out the side aisle."

Anne said, "So, that left you in charge of Will, Gilbert, Joan, Richard, and Edmund, right there in that front pew?"

"It wasn't quite like that. Edmund wasn't born yet; I was still pregnant with him. Anyway, I must have been distracted or something. As the Bishop and his procession walked by, Richard ducked out of the pew and joined them."

Anne said, "Richard? I never hear a peep out of him; he stays in his room all the time."

Joan said, "Richard was a holy terror. He always used to pinch me and scoot away."

"He was a handful. When the Bishop reached the altar, he sat down in the biggest, most important chair. Richard proceeded to stand directly in front of him, and he made this awful face. The Bishop looked a bit surprised, but quickly recovered his composure. He boomed, in loud pastoral voice: 'Well, well. What do we have here? A young squire who can hardly wait to see me?' Richard made the face even weirder, then turned so the whole church could see him. 'The Bishop leaned forward to look at Richard directly. 'Come, come lad, I don't bite. What is your name?'

Richard reached for the gold cross hanging from the Bishop's neck. The bishop drew back, and brushed Richard's hand away. Richard gave a fierce look and kicked the Bishop in the shin, hard. Then he made some strange noises and ran off toward the door."

Joan said, "His noises were peculiar. He sounded like an animal- a squirrel, maybe, but much louder."

Mother continued, "Needless to say, I grabbed Will, Gilbert, and you, Joan, and hustled out the side aisle after him. When Father heard what happened, he was mortified. He said not only would the Bishop dislike us, but it would ruin him."

"That sounds awful," said Anne. "I can see why Father would call it the start of the Shakespeare Curse."

Susanna and Judith had been playing quietly in a corner of the kitchen, but Edmund and Hamnet arriving home from school interrupted them.

Hamnet looked upset. "Mother, where is Daddy? Some boy at school said he'd never seen my Daddy, so I didn't even have one. That's not so, is it?" Hamnet said.

"Of course you have a father," Anne said. "You know he works in London. He comes home when he can."

"But, it's been so long."

Susanna said, "Don't you fear, little brother. Our Daddy will . . ."

Edmund interrupted, "You're right. Last time he was here, I heard him promise to come back soon."

Judith said, in a small voice, "Daddy's never coming back."

Mother turned to her. "Child, what a hurtful thing to say. A Shakespeare promise is forever."

Judith asked her grandmother, "What about the Shakespeare Curse?"

Chapter 7

London

1592

"Now is the winter of our discontent"
King Richard III

Londoners loved entertainments. Sports, fairs, holidays, bear baitings, dancing troubadors, and acting troupes all drew crowds. Entrepreneurs built large wooden structures just outside London's city limits to avoid regulation by the London authorities. One of these structures was The Rose. Plays were presented six afternoons a week at The Rose, three by Lord Strange's Men and three by The Admiral's Men. Each troupe put on a different play every day to attract larger audiences. If a play filled the house, they would repeat it several weeks in a row. Even with this plan, the playhouse was often half empty. It was difficult to fill 1600 seats. But, Will's play, *Henry VI Part 2,* often filled the house because many came to see it two or three times.

Immediately after finishing *Henry VI Part 2*, James set Will to work on *Part 3*. Again, there was an earlier version penned by Kit Marlowe, and Will made modifications to suit the players, especially Richard. The play was completed and approved by Tilney quickly, and performances again attracted large audiences, just as James had hoped. Londoners began to speak the name Will Shakespeare.

It was a custom among the showy gentlemen from the two or three pence seats to mill about the stage after a performance or even go into the tiring house to flatter the best players and insult the bad ones. After the third performance of *Henry VI Part 3*, two well-dressed gentlemen emerged from one of the lords' boxes and pushed their way through the lingering, noisy crowd. A hush fell over the players by the time Kit Marlowe and his dark, elegant-looking companion reached the middle of the oversized room. Most of the crowd stepped back, putting the two men at the center. Will walked over to greet them.

"Master Shakespeare, I see you borrowed a lot from a recent play of mine." Kit Marlowe took Will's hand. "But even all those battles couldn't save a tedious moment in history. At least you had the good sense not to suggest killing all the lawyers like you did in the last play. That could get you into more trouble than just boring words."

"You and I both mine Holinshed's Chronicles and Henry Hall for histories. It's no secret," said Will as he looked at the tall, wavy-haired man who stood next to Marlowe. His prominent cheekbones and a well-trimmed beard gave him a sophisticated but impish look. "Was your companion equally bored?"

"Signor John Florio loves words and was confused by some of the ones you misused."

John Florio gestured with both hands. "Master Shakespeare, your play was very good- molto bene. Your words came smoothly and fit the players well."

"Might I clear up any of the words that seem to have confused Master Marlowe?" Will said.

"Join us, please, at Southampton House this evening," John Florio said. "I'm the Earl's Italian tutor and we'll have time to talk words, words, words. I especially enjoyed your closing lines: '*Sound drums and trumpets! Farewell sour annoy! For here, I hope, begins our lasting joy.*'"

"Such naïve drivel. Come, John, we must leave." Marlowe linked his arm through Florio's. "You got to meet Shakespeare, as you wished, but I doubt the Earl would be much interested in our friend here." Marlowe snorted. "The Earl enjoys laughter, food, and women, not weighty pathos. Soon, audiences will tire of Master Shakespeare and he'll have to go back to his sheep."

Will kept his eyes on John Florio. He was intrigued by this man's ease in inviting him to the Earl's. "Thank you for the invitation, Master Florio. I'd be honored to meet the Earl, but tonight I have other plans."

"Another time, yes. And I'll tell the Earl of our conversation. Good day."

Will was pleased with the thought of someone telling an Earl about him.

The following month, the *Henry VI* series continued its rapid pace with Part 1 named for its order of occurrence in the life of King Henry.

One day shortly after performances of Part 1 had started, Will woke up early, and started for the playhouse just after first light. The day was cold and dark, but slowly moving wagons with black concealments crowded the streets. The stench was worse than usual. This didn't look good. Snow threatened as beads of rain began to soak him and he ran most of the way. When Will rounded the last corner before The Rose, he saw a crowd in front and heard angry voices.

George Bryan, a player, met him first "We've been closed down."

Behind him, a large white parchment was nailed to the door.

Proclamation

*All manner of concourse and public
meetings of the people at plays, bear-
baitings, bowlings and other like
assemblies for sports are hereby
forbidden until further notice.
By order of Her Majesty,
Queen Elizabeth*

The plague.

The heavy door creaked as James Burbage pushed it open from inside.

"Come in out of the rain." He stood at the threshold and studied all sixteen faces as they solemnly moved forward. "The plague is much worse this time. Rumor is that it has spread so quickly, the council fears it might decimate London."

"All since yesterday?" cried one of the players.

"I was unprepared for this," James said.

"Where's the Queen?"

"She left early this morning. Since no playhouse will be open, we must prepare immediately to go on tour."

"Who gets to go?" A player in back yelled.

"I need all of you to pack the props and costumes, but only four will make the tour." James let the reality sink in. "The most experienced ones. That means Kempe, Cowley, Bryan, and Richard from our troupe and four from Ned Alleyn's."

"You take those bloodsuckers instead of us?" Humphrey Jeffes said.

"Proven performers draw crowds. It's difficult to make a profit in the countryside."

"How will we live with no work?"

"I'll pay those who work today, but after that, you're on your own. God be with you." James turned and went toward the tiring house, while Richard stood in the doorway.

"I need three groups for packing," Richard said. "Costumes, props, and staging."

Will pushed through the group past Richard. "Wait, James. What about me?"

James waited for him. "I know things are difficult for you in Stratford but it's not safe here. You've got to get out. "

"My family needs what I send them, not another person to feed. Besides, it's impossible to write there."

"Sorry, nothing I can do."

As James turned, a line from the most recent play ran through Will's head: *My thoughts are whirled like a potter's wheel; I know not where I am, nor what I do;*

Chapter 8

London

January 1593

> "Shall I compare thee to a summer's day?
> Thou art more lovely and more temperate:
> Rough winds do shake the darling buds of May,
> And summer's lease hath all too short a date."
>
> *Sonnet 18*

Will left the Rose, crossed London Bridge and walked west until he arrived at Southampton House in Holborn. The servants were packing up as if to move. It wasn't hard to find John Florio.

"Why Master Shakespeare, the playwright. As you see, we are most busy. What might I do for you?"

"The plague has shut us down and I need to get away from London," Will said. "I hoped you would say something to the Earl."

"The Earl has already left, and I'm on my way to meet him at his place near Titchfield." John twisted his moustache and smiled. "Perhaps you would join me?"

"You're very kind."

"It would be interesting, but we leave within two hours. You must be ready to leave then and you cannot bring more than one trunk."

"I'll be here."

Late that afternoon, Will and John sat across from each other in a bright red coach pulled by a team of spirited horses on the journey from London. In the back of the coach, large trunks of household goods and specialties found in exclusive London shops banged against the walls, but heavy ropes secured them adequately. Inside the elegant coach, there was plenty of room for John and Will. They headed for Place House, the former Titchfield Abbey, near Southampton. This grand estate served as the main residence of Henry Wriothesley, third Earl of Southampton.

As the coach jostled along, Will put both hands around his middle to keep his insides from tumbling out. He wanted to relax on the soft velvet cushion, but every bump in the road jolted his stomach and his mind to the events of the last day.

John simply rolled with each new bounce. How the coach stayed together was testament to the skill of its builder. It dropped into deep ruts, tipped on fast curves and bumped over enormous tree roots. Will's nostrils were assaulted by the odor of wet earth, horse sweat, and decaying foliage found in damp woods during the heat of summer. The taste of bile rose in his throat. He perspired heavily.

"You look sick, Master Shakespeare," John said. "Perhaps it would be wise to stop at the next inn."

"I think we should continue, but it's kind of you to offer, Master Florio. My stomach is more accustomed to staying in one place."

"Bene, bene- Please call me John. Poor man. One grows accustomed to the southern roads after a few trips. Let's just hope the mud doesn't get so bad we'll have to get out and push." John looked out the window and pointed. "This part is the worst. It is best to relax and think of other things until we are past."

"I'll try that as best I can. Perhaps you can tell me about the Earl. What's he like?"

John raised both eyebrows. "The answer is not simple. Many would say the Earl is difficult, and he's not even twenty yet. His mother, The Countess and his guardian, the Queen's Secretary of State, William Cecil would agree. But the Earl of Essex would call him delightful and fun-loving. You see, it's not so simple to describe my Earl." John twirled his mustache and grinned. "I think they all describe him correctly, depending."

"On what?"

"The way he feels at the moment. But don't worry about yourself, the Earl already likes you."

"How would you know that? We've never met."

"Ah, but you're a writer, and the Earl loves writers. He and Kit Marlowe get along famously."

John reached under his seat and pulled out a basket of food. "The color has returned to your face. Have some fruit or cakes."

"You're most gracious, but my stomach still needs calm." Will watched John unwrap a lemon biscuit cake and take a small bite. "I want to know more about the Earl. What is his life like here?"

"He spends a lot of his time at Queen Elizabeth's court, but in plague times, he comes to Place House, or hunts and sails at the Palace at Beaulieu, close by." John ran his tongue over his lips to clean off the powdered sugar. "Both are his family's country estates. You'll find them most enjoyable."

"Do you often invite people to the Earl's estates?"

"Not often." John laughed. "Although he trusts me implicitly, he believes I spy for his mother."

"Then, will he think I'm a spy?"

"He knows about you. He and Marlowe talk about you."

"Quite so; and what do they say?"

"They argue about your plays."

"They're friends?"

"Maybe more than that. They argue all the time. You know Kit; his influence might encourage the Earl to do something really stupid and never achieve adulthood. The Earl loves a good time and drives his mother crazy with his outrageous behavior. She would like me to surround him with more stable influences. I think you fit that description perfectly."

The road finally became less bumpy. Will leaned back in his seat.

That night, they stopped at a small inn where the sack was plentiful and Will slept well next to John Florio in spite of the scratchy straw and crowded conditions. The next morning, they left at dawn and arrived at Place House by early afternoon. The estate was originally built as a monastery before it was given to the Earl's grandfather by King Henry

VIII. In its history, it withstood many attacks because it was made of heavy stone, but none were as noteworthy as the series of parties the present Earl threw. Even though his mother and guardian placed him on a limited allowance, he managed to drain a substantial portion of his inheritance.

As soon as the coach approached, word spread so a group of neatly dressed servants were waiting in the estate entrance when they arrived. Two tall dark towers flanked the fortress-like house and the sight of it intrigued Will with thoughts of what might be taking place inside.

When the coach stopped, three servants took the trunks and two more greeted John. Will was introduced as a London playwright. A servant-girl, Helene, giggled when she heard he was a London playwright. One of the other servants joined in her laughter. "I can see you're different from the last one."

Another servant said to Will, "I'm here to take you up to your room. You will be right next to Master Florio. Before the Earl returns, best you take some time to meet everyone and see the grounds. Once he arrives, there'll be no idle time."

Within the hour, the cook served dinner in the kitchen to Will and John, who insisted the house servants join them. They ate poultry, veal and game, fresh cabbage and lettuce salads, summer carrots, spinach, garlic, skirret, freshly-picked peaches, oranges, pomegranates, and warm breads. It was more food than Will had ever seen at one meal. Helene kept their glasses filled with a smooth, sweet white wine.

The servants' conversation reminded Will of friends from Stratford and he caught himself making comparisons. After dinner, he went to his room to write down a few thoughts. The wash bowl was filled for a second time with fresh water. He soon fell asleep on the most comfortable bed he had ever slept on.

The next day, Will began to explore the thousands of acres and buildings that were on the estate. He met some of the day servants who lived in town and others who lived just outside the walls of the manor house with their families.

Dinner was again served in the kitchen, this time with more hot meats than before. "The Earl serves the best sack, does he not?" John said, as he raised his glass high.

Will smiled, "It appears I don't drink from this glass, as it's always full. I hesitate to enjoy too much, lest my wits desert me when the Earl arrives."

"We never know when he'll appear, or what he'll do when he gets here." John downed another goblet of sack. "When he's away, I enjoy as much of life here as I can."

Just then, they heard a shout, and a young girl ran into the kitchen, "The Earl has been sighted an hour away."

John stood. "He'll expect us all to greet him the moment he arrives." The others quickly finished their meal and went to work making everything tidy and perfect. Within the hour, they joined the servants standing at attention in the great entry hall.

In minutes, a small and delicately featured young man strode through the opened doorway. When he removed his riding hat, long auburn curls tumbled down past his shoulders. He brushed wisps of hair from his eyes before he met John's gaze. Will marveled at this handsome, yet delicate creature. Unlike the male actors who dressed as elegant women, the Earl wore no make-up or wig. He was the most beautiful man Will had ever seen. What a great player he would make.

"Is my estate in good order, John?" The Earl asked in a tone that was clearly in charge.

"Quite so, your lordship," John said. "I hope your travels went well," The Earl handed his riding hat to John. "Yes, yes, it was quite merry." The Earl yawned. "What news from London?"

"The plague rages, but I brought you a special guest. This is William Shakespeare, the poet and playwright I enticed to furnish some entertainments here."

Will stepped forward. "My lord, this is indeed an honor."

"Yes, yes, I pray John did not entice you with promises I know nothing about. Tell me your name again. John's accent always mangles names."

"Shakespeare, William Shakespeare. My friends call me Will."

"Very well." He turned toward the dining hall and shouted. "Get me some sack. Now John, why is this fellow here?"

"He's a London play maker. But the playhouses are closed..."

"Of course, I know that. That's why I'm here. Mother and Lord Cecil wouldn't allow me anywhere near London. I suppose we could put on some plays here. It might be amusing. Bring Master Shagsper to the library."

Soon, they were all seated in the large, book-lined room that was warmed by a huge stone fireplace. The servant, Helene, stood close behind, ready to pour the Earl's sack.

Will again scanned the leather-bound volumes that filled the shelves while he waited for the Earl to settle himself. "Your collection of literary treasures amazes me. You have the best imaginable, in all languages, especially Italian."

The Earl shot a glance at John. "Indeed. While you're here, read any you like. They are the pride of my family," the Earl said. "Now I need something to eat."

Helene left immediately, and returned in short order with a silver tray piled with platters of meats, fish, cheese, fruits, breads and more wine. The Earl watched her carefully as she set down the food and once more stood to the side.

The Earl took a bite. "Don't hover so."

John watched her move to the entrance and nodded his approval. "Helene started just before you left with Master Marlowe. I hope you're pleased."

"Yes," the Earl said. He chewed the crusty bread. "On my way here, I found the countryside crowded with Londoners fleeing the plague. We'll undoubtedly encounter all manner of guests in the months to come. They'll need entertainment."

Will said, "Your lordship, I also act in plays and write poetry. Perhaps John Florio showed you the poem I gave him a while ago, *Venus and Adonis*." Will watched the Earl's smooth face for some sign of recognition.

"You remember, your lordship, it was the long one, written by hand," John said.

The Earl stood. Holding the wine in one hand he turned to them.

"'Fondling,' she saith,
'since I have hemm'd thee here within the circuit of this ivory
pale,
    I'll be a park, and thou shalt be my deer;
    Feed where thou wilt, on mountain or in dale;
    Graze on my lips; and if those hills be dry,
    Stray lower, where the pleasant fountains lie."

He gulped his wine. "As you can see, I remember your work. I think I'll like having you here."

"Your performance honors me," Will said.

"It's a magnificent poem. Why, for a while, I could quote much longer passages," the Earl said. "Master Florio here thinks of me as some kind of Adonis, so he must have thought the poem about me."

"Your lordship, you know I . . ."

"Yes, I know. Let someone with talent speak. Tell me, could I be some kind of Adonis?"

"Your lordship might resemble Adonis in appearance, but I hope you experience a different end to your story. Adonis lost his life in a brutal way without pure love or heirs. That would hardly seem suitable for you."

"My mother couldn't have said it better. However, I like your honeyed words and quiet ways. You know, I have some writing experience myself. At Cambridge, I penned many essays, and a few short poems. It was a pleasant pastime." He leaned back in the chair. "Now tell me, what are your plans since the playhouses are closed?"

"I hope to have *Venus and Adonis* published, write more poems and perhaps even some plays."

"You're quite ambitious and I admire a person who knows what he wants. With London uninhabitable, where do you plan to live?"

"I have no definite plans."

"Sometimes, my Italian tutor likes to influence me. It's Mother's idea, right, John? No matter. Will, might you spend some time here, writing poems or plays for me and my guests?"

"I would be honored." Will sat up straight in his chair. "You find poetry a pleasant leisure activity, and I find it much more than that. Perhaps it would add interest if we also exchanged sonnets."

The Earl raised his eyebrows. "Oh, that is wonderfully rich. The poet who requires the patron to write. I like it. John, arrange it. Also, dismiss the serving girl. She was inattentive." The Earl strode from the room.

Life at Place House was never routine. Sometimes the Earl demanded Italian lessons at midnight, often he slept all morning, and every day he required a huge dinner, served at different hours in the afternoon. He insisted on at least one sonnet every day from Will, who obliged with honest observations of the Earl's life:

Is it for fear to wet a widow's eye
That thou consum'st thyself in single life?
Ah! if thou issueless shalt hap to die,
the world will wail thee like a makeless wife;
The world will be thy widow and still weep,
That thou no form of thee hast left behind,
When every private widow well may keep,
By children's eyes, her husband's shape in mind
Look what an unthrift in the world doth spend
Shifts but his place, for still the world enjoys it;
But beauty's waste hath in the world an end,
And kept unus'd, the user so destroys it.
No love toward others in that bosom sits
That on himself such murd'rous shame commits.

The Earl's responses were sporadic and highly varied. Sometimes he dramatized his effort by reading at the top of his voice, punctuating certain parts with grand theatrical gestures. Other times he had a servant deliver a sonnet to Will in the middle of the night. Some consisted of a few lines, scrawled on a page torn from a book. Others showed reasonable effort.

In this sonnet, I address the spirit
Of my elders who prompt me to marry:
Your wise words of advice strongly m'ir it,
Telling me much too long do I tarry.
From your lofty perch, you 'say I need help
As I live my life much too dreamily,
Behaving poorly, almost like a whelp,
Since I'm not yet starting a family.
But my inmost soul craves grand adventure,
So settling down is not yet apropos,
But when 'tis, I'll gladly choose indenture,
And seek calm, comfortable status quo.
As poesy goes, this may sound heady,
but, like the Gordian, I'm just not ready.

Henry Wriothesley
Third Earl of Southampton
Baron of Titchfield

Sometimes, the Earl confessed serious concerns to Will about his useless life and his family's attitude toward him as if they were confidants, but when guests were around he completely ignored him. On a moment's notice, he would insist Will accompany him to a favored tavern, on a hunting expedition, or a sailing trip. Other times, the Earl would vanish by himself for several days, leaving the house staff suddenly free to do as they pleased. Then he would return without explanation and resume as if he had never left.

The Earl was gone often enough that Will found plenty of time to write. He spent hours reading books from the Earl's library, and talking to John Florio. He walked outside daily, regardless of the weather.

One late Autumn day, Will and John strolled through the gardens enjoying the cool weather and rich color of the late flowers without the Earl's distraction.

Will laughed at John's latest question. "Yes, the English love to use shortened versions of people's names. We call Henry, Harry; Richard, Dick; Christopher, Kit; Robert, Robin; Edward, Ned; Mary, Moll; and many others. People enjoy these nicknames." John sat down and scribbled in his book.

"Also, Catholics use Latin words and names to talk in code," John said.

"Catholics, what do you know about them? I thought you were a good Protestant."

"What, like you?"

"I attend church at all the right times."

"Back home in Stratford, maybe. But you don't go to church very often in London."

"It's not easy to make money, you know."

"True, but what about your family's strong Catholic connections?"

"Those are my mother's distant relatives, and I never paid much attention to them. How do you know so much about my family?"

"I'm a good listener, and people tell me things."

"Well, I'll tell you this: I've got too much on my mind to even think about religion. My father felt the same. He humored my mother's relatives, but then hid the writings they gave him. If the wrong people ever found them,..."

Will heard the sound of a coach, so they walked quickly around the outside wall, where they could see the front entrance. Two men spilled from the carriage, laughing. Both required a groomsman's arm to right them.

"By cock and pie," Will said. "You never know how he'll be when he shows up."

"Nor what he's liable to do."

They watched the Earl lurch toward the entrance, towing his guest.

John put his notebook away. "We'd best go help them."

As soon as they got close, the Earl threw his arms around John. "I brought my friend, Kit Marlowe."

Kit bowed and almost fell. He nodded to Will. "The country playwright, Master Shakespur." He belched. "If you and John are thick as thieves, the Earl should beware."

"Your words sound like the mutterings of a malt-worm," Will said.

"What poet insults his patron's friend?" Kit farted. "I'd replace him."

"Kit and I have a plan." The Earl snickered. "I'll send your money to your wives."

Will looked at John.

"You need no money," the Earl said. "I supply everything here."

"There'll be no joy among the money-lenders today." Marlowe doubled over with laughter.

"Now Kit and I are leaving." The Earl burped. "Go back to your words unless you'd rather go to London to check the plague's progress personally."

John and Will watched them stumble up the stairs while two nervous servants walked behind them in case they fell. John tugged at Will's arm. "Let's be gone from their sight before they come up with more ideas."

"Will he really send them the money?"

"Don't worry. His mother will see to it."

"Do you think Marlowe wants to be here instead of me?"

"Not at all. He would be here if he wanted. He likes to stir up trouble and watch people squirm. His plays are good and Londoners adore him. As long as he's popular, the Earl will want his company."

"I don't think this house is big enough for all of us," Will said.

"Don't worry. They'll soon leave for some new adventure."

Two days later, after sobering up, they did exactly that.

In January, Will received a letter from Gilbert about the money the Earl sent. He was relieved. Marlowe's subsequent visits were short but frequent and Will spent as much time as possible in his room reading and writing or on long walks in the countryside. Then, in May, Marlowe's visits suddenly ceased and the Earl sent for John and Will every day to walk with him and help plan a new garden.

The weather was lovely. A warm afternoon sun chased the morning coolness and dried the dew, making it easy to walk through the woods. The Earl reached over and snapped the stem of the tallest lily. He twirled it between two fingers. "If I tell a lady that I admire her bosom, she takes offense. If I tell that same lady that the cut of her gown pleases me, she's enchanted."

Will reached for the flower. "Don't overlook the manner she chooses for those thanks."

John raised his hand to object. "In these matters, the Italians far exceed the English."

"Especially in the matter of the bosom," the Earl said.

A servant approached and curtsied. "Pardon me, Your Lordship. Robert Devereaux, The Earl of Essex, has arrived on horseback from London. He waits in the main hall."

"Bring him out here at once." The Earl rubbed his hands together and turned to Will and John. "I'm eager for court gossip and the latest military strategies."

Essex emerged from the house, dressed in clothes as black as his hair, feathered hat in hand and sword at his hip. His height and powerful build were accentuated by a long brown beard. He surveyed the garden quickly before joining the group.

The Earl hugged Essex. "My warmest greetings, Robert. You look harried. I'll have some refreshments brought out for you."

"Greetings, Harry. You observe me well." He nodded to John, but looked at Will. "And who might this be?."

"This is Will Shakespeare. He writes poems and plays," the Earl said.

Essex said, "Send them away. We need to talk about Sir Stink."

The Earl blanched. "Let's go inside." He turned back toward Will and John. "Make arrangements for this evening's entertainment."

"As you wish," John said. They went toward the side garden entrance.

"Who is Sir Stink?" Will asked.

"That's what they call Sir Walter Raleigh because of his constant smoking of that plant leaf called tobacco."

"How are they involved with Raleigh?"

John looked toward the house and saw both Earls enter the library. He stopped. "Quickly, come with me and don't make any noise."

John led Will into the house and through a small doorway. He removed the burning wall torch and lit their way down some stairs into a low tunneled hallway. There was a tiny damp room at the end where a single bench stood against the far wall.

"This looks like a cell. What is it?"

"Shh. You'll know soon enough. Here, hold this torch, so I can see," whispered John, as he moved the bench to the corner.

Will held the torch while John stood on the bench and felt along the wall where it joined the ceiling. Finally, he pulled out a brick. Will could hear muffled voices. John removed a second brick, and the voices became clearer. He motioned Will to stand next to him on the bench.

When Will climbed up, he heard the voice of Essex, "So, with our friend out of the way, we won't be able to embarrass Raleigh in the eyes of the Queen."

The Earl's distinctive voice answered, "That bastard! How I would love to see the Queen rack him for the treasonous scoundrel he is."

"Our revenge will require patience. Right now, you must get out of here because Raleigh has the Queen's favor, and he might believe you're part of the plot against him. He could have his men provoke an incident the way they did to our friend in Deptford."

"But Robert," the Earl said, "I never get into trouble. John's my constant protector. He steps in and extracts me before anything happens. Now he brings Will along, and the two of them keep my life miserably boring. They follow me everywhere."

"Don't be foolish. Your tutor and playwright are no match for Raleigh's secret army. I'm at court every day, and I know these things. You must be far away from Raleigh's men for my sake as well as yours."

Will whispered, "What is this about?"

John put his finger to his lips.

Essex continued. "Promise me your departure will be quick, Harry. I must return to London immediately before I'm missed at court. I only left because I couldn't trust this news to a messenger."

"Very well. I'll do as you say."

"You haven't a choice."

"How shall we communicate while I travel?"

John reached for the bricks and quickly eased them back in place. He jumped off the bench, and whispered, "Out of here, quickly."

They ran back to the hallway and put out the torch.

"You must be a spy," Will said.

"You sound like one of those Puritans talking about plays."

"You know what I mean. It's deceitful."

"It's necessary. I need to know everything I can, because I have concerns that you know nothing about."

"But the Earl seems to trust you completely. How did you two get to be so close?"

"That's way too long a story for right now. I have the Earl's best interests at heart, and if you do too, you'll keep quiet about what you just saw and heard. Believe me, it's in your best interests also."

"Is that a threat?"

"It's good advice from a friend. Now, let's hurry and return to the garden. The Earl will look for us to set his plans in motion."

They walked only a short distance in the garden before the Earl approached. "The Earl of Essex left, and we must prepare for departure ourselves. John, you always wanted me to go to Italy with you, and tomorrow we'll do just that. In fact, we'll stay several months, so we'll take half the servants." He turned to Will. "You know how this place works. You stay here and manage the estate. Send your sonnets by messenger."

"I, I, I . . . As you wish. Perhaps I'll finish *The Rape of Lucrece*."

"One more thing, Will. If anyone inquires about my sudden departure, tell them it is a long-planned trip." The Earl rubbed his eyes. "Stupid court politics have caused the death of our good friend, Kit Marlowe. He was killed in a tavern in Deptford last week."

Will gasped. "Marlowe? Dead?"

"Ruffians provoked a fight and stabbed him through the eye." The Earl shuddered. "Come, John, let's make haste before I become any more upset."

As they walked away, John turned toward Will and shrugged his shoulders.

Will's mind raced to the different possibilities. Would the Earl expect him to replace Marlowe in their adventures. Would he abandon all poets? How might this change his life?

Chapter 9

Place House, Titchfield

1594

"Though this be madness, yet there is method in 't."
Hamlet

Managing the estate in the Earl's absence didn't require much of Will's time unless a guest arrived. Then he had to act as host and assign servants to assist in making their visit comfortable. He followed the suggestions of the housekeeper, cook and estate steward who enjoyed their elevated status with Will. Because of the plague in London and peace on the continent, many travelers stopped on their way to nearby Portsmouth. This created a flow of people away from London as well as a need for couriers to get messages and goods back there.

Shortly after the Earl's departure, an unusual traveler stopped at Place House. A woman behind a dark veil with an elegant cape that matched her stylish hat emerged from an well-appointed coach and asked to see the lord of the manor. Will greeted her in the large entryway, "Welcome to Place House, Madame. I am at a disadvantage because I do not know your name, but I am . . ."

"I know some things about you. You are Henry Wriothesley, 3rd Earl of Southampton, but I am not going to reveal who I am." The lady extended her hand and Will took it while keeping his eyes on her hidden face.

"That's a handicap for me," said Will.

"You'll see why. I was sent by one of the Queen's attendants on a rather delicate and secretive matter, and my identity is unimportant."

"To be fair, perhaps my true identity should also be unknown."

The lady laughed. "I thought you would have longer hair, but already, I like you for your sense of humor. I'll pretend I don't know who you are. May I stay a while to get to know you further?"

Will also laughed. "Appearances can be deceiving. I see no reason why you should not visit a while. However, how am I to address you if you have no name?"

She took off her hat and veil and revealed coal black hair with matching dark eyes. Her loosened cape revealed a slim but well-proportioned figure. "Call me the Dark Lady."

Will was struck by her ravishing beauty and radiant smile. "The Dark Lady it is, then. And I shall be The Poet."

"Oh, are you really a poet?"

"I have been known to write some. If you stay a while, perhaps you will see some evidence of my abilities."

"That would be lovely, and I might respond in kind."

Extending the Earl's hospitality had become almost second nature for Will, so it took little effort to accommodate this new guest. She retired to her room adjacent to Will's to wash up from the ride and take a short nap before dressing in evening clothes. This gave Will a chance to alert the servants about his ruse. They met again in the dining room where the two of them sat at the ends of a long table.

"Tell me, do you get to see any plays in London?" said Will, affecting his best Earlish behavior.

"A few, but I mostly read. I generally favor plays by Kit Marlowe, although I heard an ugly rumor about him recently. Do you know him?"

"Only by reputation. Have you heard of William Shakespeare?"

"Was he the one that was called an upstart Crow by Robert Greene?"

"That's the one. He hasn't been writing long."

"Didn't he write a series of plays about Henry VI? Too many battles for me. I heard they were gruesome."

"Well, let's have no gruesome battles while you're visiting."

"Agreed."

The Earl's servants were quite practiced, and provided excellent food and wine right on cue. Will and the Dark Lady ate heartily, and went for a walk after dinner.

Will asked, "Are you familiar with the form of poetry called sonnets?"

"Yes, they are my favorite kind of poems."

"Well, if we finish our walk soon, I'll write a sonnet for you and have it ready by morning."

"That would be lovely."

When they returned to Place House, Will retired to the study and the Dark Lady to her room. She had no idea he was next door. Will chuckled at the servants' audacity.

In the morning, the Dark Lady awakened to find a hand-written sonnet under her door:

In the old age black was not counted fair,
Or if it were, it bore not beauty's name;
But now is black beauty's successive heir,
And beauty slandered with a bastard shame:
For since each hand hath put on Nature's power,
Fairing the foul with Art's false borrowed face,
Sweet beauty hath no name, no holy bower,
But is profaned, if not lives in disgrace.
Therefore my mistress' eyes are raven black,
Her eyes so suited, and they mourners seem
At such who, not born fair, no beauty lack,
Sland'ring creation with a false esteem:
Yet so they mourn becoming of their woe,
That every tongue says beauty should look so.

How magnificent, she thought. She took quill in hand and began scratching on foolscap. When she finished, even before breakfast, this was the result:

For me to compete
With a fellow so dear
Could lead to a beat that might sound queer.
But try I must
Or fail I will
So even with rust,
My words won't fall ill.
Your brown eyes see all
Admitting no shame.
There is no wall,
Not in your name.
So then, brave poet,
You have seed, so sow it.

At breakfast, Will said, "I've never met a woman with such skills."

"That barely touches all I have to offer," she said.

Through the next day, they enjoyed meals, long talks about people they knew but not known to each other and long walks around the Earl's estate. As they explored, Will slipped his hand into hers, and she accepted eagerly. Some hours after they retired for the evening, Will heard small sounds from the room next door. He knocked lightly, and the door opened almost immediately.

Will said, "Are you having difficulties?"

The Dark Lady said, "I can't seem to fall asleep."

"Neither can I," said Will.

She opened the door wider. Her night clothes were in disarray, and it reminded Will of Anne- attractive and vulnerable. Will gulped.

"Perhaps we think too much about sonnet rhymes." She grabbed Will's arm and pulled him into the room, pushing herself against him while she started pulling up the back of his night shirt.

Will put his arms around her and found her quite warm. She continued pulling his shirt until she had it over his head. She then drew him towards the bed and molded his half-naked body to hers. Thoughts of Anne danced in Will's mind, but they were fleeting and were overpowered by longing.

Many hours later, Will returned to his room. Thoughts whirled in his head, too complicated to sort out. New sonnets began to form, then dissolve into visions of Anne. The jumble continued for a long time before he finally fell asleep.

The next day both of them felt strong emotions and could hardly stay away from each other. For almost a month they shared meals and walks with only afternoon breaks when Will went to the library to write. Every night after the house became quiet, Will went to her room. Her passion took him beyond any feeling he had ever experienced. She filled him with a joy that made his heart swell. He could barely think beyond her presence.

This continued for almost a month. Then the Earl and John showed up, unannounced. It all came to a grinding halt.

John strode in first, ostensibly to check the condition of the house. When he spied the Dark Lady, he blanched visibly and pulled Will aside.

"Will, you must leave. Now." Will had never seen John so agitated.

The Earl was right behind. "Yes, Will. While John sorts things out, go to Beaulieu and catch up on your writing, like that play I asked you to write for my mother's wedding. You seem to have become distracted."

Will said, "But you haven't even met our guest."

"No need of that," said John. "Things are not always as they seem. Go now. The servants will follow with your things."

The Dark Lady looked down, not meeting Will's glance.

Although he was angry at being dismissed so rudely, Will could see that any protest would be futile. He left, looking back only once to find no one watching his departure. John and the Earl were speaking intently to the Dark Lady.

Will walked to the stable, confused and dismayed. He knew from John's demeanor that it would not be a pleasant scene at Place House. Besides, the Earl was actually correct: Will was falling behind in his writing.

Beaulieu Palace offered a fine place for Will to write. There were fewer rooms but they were all large and elegantly decorated with beautifully carved wooden furniture and leather and velvet covered chairs and sofas. Every room centered around a huge fireplace surrounded with layered heavy wood. Beaulieu's library wasn't nearly as extensive as Place House, but Will had his few books from the Earl's main library and mined the works of Plutarch and Ovid for stories. His rooms were more than adequate, the grounds and nearby woods lush, and Beaulieu's reputation as being haunted minimized unwanted visitors. The staff was small, but quite competent.

The servants who brought his things included all the notes and books that had been in his room. For this, he was grateful. Besides the desperately-needed quiet, the accommodations were as pleasing as Titchfield had been. Although often distracted by thoughts about the Dark Lady, he got a good start on a comedy about a wedding that featured not only the happy couple, but local handymen putting on a play, and a forest full of fairies who played various tricks. He even found a treasure of a book that told about a person transformed into a donkey, and a wonderful fairy named, Puck. Progress was quite swift for a few weeks, but Will ran into a block that stopped him cold. He couldn't stop wondering if the dark lady brought him real love or a banquet for a starving traveler. There was no comparing her to Anne, for he could not forget the progression of his feelings for Anne from first love through the birth of their children and the angst of their separation

To get himself back into writing, he sent word to John that he needed a book, Plautus, from the Earl's library, and he wanted John to deliver it personally.

John wasted no time, and came the next day. At dinner Will asked about the episode with the Dark Lady at Titchfield.

"I hope I did not offend the Earl with that business . . ."

John grimaced. "You weren't the offending party. I'm sorry you got tangled up in that, but you did exactly the right thing by departing. It's all taken care of now, so there's nothing to worry about."

"It doesn't sound like I'm going to learn more about it, then."

"You understand me perfectly. I brought the book you wanted in hopes it will help your play for our Earl's mother."

"Thanks. I also need your help with that very play."

"Me? That's rich. My Italian is pretty good, but English still mystifies me at times."

Will laughed. "You're not alone there. I don't need your help with any Italian just yet. What I want you to do, is to read aloud some lines from the play."

Will gave him several sheets of foolscap. "I have Richard Burbage read lines for me sometimes to see how strong they sound. Start here."

John spoke the lines:

We will meet; and there we may rehearse most obscenely and courageously.
Take pains; be perfect: adieu.

"Next."

I pray you, commend me to Mistress Squash, your mother, and to Master Peascod, your father. Good Master Peaseblossom, I shall desire you of more acquaintance too. Your name, I beseech you, sir?

"John, more feeling."

I see a voice: now will I to the chink,
To spy an I can hear my Thisby's face. Thisby!

"It's no use. This play is way too flat. The plot and characters are fine, but just hearing the lines in my mind's eye is not good enough and I can't fix them to please the audience unless Richard Burbage reads for me." Will buried his head in his hands. If only he could imagine Richard's voice reading the lines. But it just never happened. What was wrong with him? Why did the voice of his character have to come from the performer?

John said, "Your play-within-a-play idea is quite appealing. The audience will be entertained. But I thought you would be busy writing elegant sonnets and poems like the great masters of old."

"But who would support me? Can you see me writing at the whim of a patron like the Earl? I don't have the university education or financial support to earn my keep."

"Don't sell yourself short. You are an excellent writer."

"Your praise is welcome, and indeed, I can write. Give me classic stories to adapt and Richard Burbage to speak the lines, and I can write plays to entertain everyone."

"But, the plague . . ."

"Either it will abate or we're all dead, so it won't matter anyway."

"Your logic is ugly, but inescapable. I'll tell the Earl you are making progress on the play for his mother. And feel free to toss plot ideas at me."

"John, you may save me."

"You know how I love words. And plots are high in my interest, thanks to the Earl."

"One of the Earl's books concerns a comedy set in Italy, called *The Taming of the Shrew*. Taming a wife is always amusing, but I need some help with the Italian aspects."

John gave Will a suspicious look. "Why ask me about taming a wife?"

"Well, you offered . . ."

John relaxed a bit. "Indeed. My wary nature doesn't always serve me well. It would please me to assist you."

"Shall I call for you every time I want your help?"

"No need. I will check in with you every week at least."

Several weeks later, Will confirmed that the Earl was home, and made the short journey to Place House.

"Ah, Will, so good to see you. I've been busy with plans for my birthday."

"I have several sonnets and two plays for your lordship, one of which is for your mother's wedding."

"You never disappoint. I owe you a great deal of thanks. Now that I'm about to become an official adult, thanks to you and John, I finally know what I have to do. The trip to Italy with John and that awkwardness before you went to Beaulieu opened my eyes to the important things in life."

"Oh, really. Tell me what you think."

"Your sonnets spoke so effectively about love that I know I cannot engage in an arranged marriage. My guardian, Lord Cecil wants me to marry his eldest granddaughter, Elizabeth de Vere. Her father, the 17th Earl of Oxford, had also been a ward of Lord Cecil, but left just before I arrived. Interesting fellow, but even worse with money than me. He wrote some good poetry for the Queen. Perhaps you've seen it in my library."

"Yes, they are quite interesting."

"My mother thinks Elizabeth de Vere would be a brilliant match, but I do not love her. Even though there are financial penalties, I know I must seek real love, wherever it takes me. Isn't that the way you married your wife?"

"Yes, that is true, but . . ."

"Oh, my truest poet and friend, you give the best advice. I want you to take some money I have planned to give you and go home to love your wife and family. This is the life you have so often advised me to aim for." The Earl went to his library and came back with a heavy bag of gold coins. "Enjoy your life, and think of me often."

"This leather pouch is heavy with your generosity. I shall never forget my time with you. Let us have one dinner together and I shall leave for Stratford tomorrow." The Earl and the poet hugged.

Will took the money, and, after sending servants to Beaulieu to get his things, went upstairs to pack the rest of his belongings. His return to Stratford would be sweet, indeed.

Chapter 10

Stratford

Early Spring 1594

"A little more than kin, and less than kind."
Hamlet

The Earl's coach pulled up to the Shakespeare house on Henley Street late in the afternoon. The day was cloudy but cool. Soon, the spring rains would begin. If Father looked out the shop window, he would see the arrival of the Earl's grand coach. Perhaps for a moment he would think a wealthy client sought his gloves or his skill at deal-making, but then he would see it was Will, and he would wonder.

Will stepped down from the coach and saw the top of his father's head as he bent over his workbench probably tracing glove patterns on leather in a tight configuration so few scraps would be left. But Father never looked up or saw the coach. Will felt a knot forming in his stomach. If Gilbert were in the shop, he would have been outside by now. How disappointing. Will went straight for the kitchen where he knew he would find the women.

Susanna saw him first, and jumped up with a scream before she hugged him tight. "Daddy, Daddy. I thought about you today. I knew you'd be here."

Anne wiped her hands on her apron and wiped a tear from her cheek. She took both his hands. "Let me look at you. It's been too long."

"I know." He pulled her close. "I've missed you so."

"You're here now and that's what counts," Mother said. She continued peeling the potatoes while she watched everyone.

Will walked over and leaned down to kiss her. Then he knelt next to Judith, who was sitting on the floor by Mother's chair, sorting beans. "No words for a tired traveler?"

"I thought you were never coming back," Judith said.

"Well, you were wrong. Touch me, I'm not a ghost." Will picked her up, to give her a hug. She was light and smaller than he remembered.

Judith hugged him as tightly as she could. "When Hamnet gets home, I get to tell him first that you're here."

"You do that. Now tell me where I can find your Uncle Gilbert."

Mother looked up. "In Shottery again. You can meet him on the road if you head that way now. Girls, we have food to cook up."

"If we get all this done soon, maybe your father will tell us stories about his travels," said Anne.

"And I want to hear some tales about what I've missed here," Will said. "I'll be back before Hamnet gets home."

Will ran toward the road to Shottery. It wasn't far. Even with the low sun glaring in his eyes, he could see Gilbert kicking a stone down the path. Will laughed. Gilbert had kicked stones from one end of Warwickshire to the other. He pulled the heavy purse from inside the folds of his shirt, tossed it toward Gilbert and yelled. "Heads up. There's danger on the road."

Gilbert looked up as the bag whizzed toward him. "God's bodkin, Will. What are you throwing at me?"

They hugged. "See what I've brought to ease your gloom," Will said.

Gilbert picked up the heavy bag and untied it. "Where did you get all this? That's more money than I've ever seen."

"More than our schoolmaster earns in three years. It's from the Earl for watching his estate while he was away and watching him when he wasn't away."

"I thought you wrote plays . . ."

"Watching the Earl wasn't hard work. I had plenty of time to write plays, so I did that too."

"All I do is work and the money just disappears into Father's hands. I can't figure what he does with it."

"Maybe he hides it in the rafters."

"We've gone without food, so I doubt it. Better not show him that bag."

"Is business that bad?"

"Not good at all. He's mortgaged Mother's property in Wilmcote to one of the Lambert cousins, Mother's taken up embroidering things for the neighbors, and he demands every farthing I bring in from wool sales." Gilbert kicked the stone.

"You think if I gave him this money it would disappear?"

"That's exactly what I think."

"After what I went through to get this, there's no way I'll turn it over to him." Will kicked Gilbert's stone. "But I do have to tell him about it."

"It's wretched around here. Edmund wants to go to London and be like you."

"Does Father ever say anything about me?"

"Only when Edmund loses his temper and yells that he's going to London."

"How do you stay here?" Will asked.

"What else could I do? Besides, if I left, the rest of them would be completely at Father's mercy."

"I want to give this money to the family to make life here easier."

"It's your money, but I am certain Father wouldn't use it for what you intend."

"You're probably right. Let's walk by school. Maybe we can catch Hamnet."

"You go ahead. I don't want to irritate Father by being late."

Will turned off the road and walked up to the bakery at Sheep and High. He had some time to see Hamnet and Judith Sadler. With all their children and a bakery to run, they were always home. He found them washing clothes in back. Once more, Judith was huge with child.

"You look about to fall into that tub," Will said. "Perhaps you're carrying twins?"

Hamnet dried his hands on his floured apron and gave Will a bear hug. "Did you think only you could have twins?"

"You are a sight for sore eyes," Judith said. "You look well."

"You've been heartily missed," Hamnet said.

"It was too long to be away from family. I hope I will never have to spend another plague time in the south country."

"Hamnet usually stops here on his way from school. He's a good boy, and attentive to his godparents," Hamnet said.

"We encourage him to talk about you, as does Anne," Judith said. "And he obliges."

"You're so good for him and I'm grateful to you for your attention."

Just then, Hamnet Shakespeare rounded the corner, and let out a loud shout. "Daddy, daddy. I knew you were coming soon. I told John Lambert. No one believed me."

"Look at you," Will said. "So big I could mistake you for a man."

"Grandpa doesn't think so. He says I speak with a boy's foolishness."

"Let's go home and you can tell me all that is on your mind. I have much to learn."

They said their good-byes to the Sadlers and left.

"Are you home for good?" young Hamnet asked.

"We'll have to see about that. Now do me a favor before we walk in the house. Let me hide and you walk in alone. Pretend you haven't seen me yet."

"Who are we fooling with this game?"

"We're pleasing Judith. Now run along and keep our secret."

The family spent the next week showing Will everything they had saved for him. They talked about their lives, their worries, and their dreams. He helped around the house and filled the women's imagination with stories of life with the Earl and at Titchfield. He didn't tell about all the things that happened there.

Some nights, when he wasn't tired, he went to the workshop and wrote. He was still working on that marriage play for the Countess Southampton. Edmund, Susanna, and the twins were curious about the play he was writing, so Sunday evening he showed it to them and had them read some of it with him. Of course, only the boys could read and

Susanna was furious that she was left out. Will saved some lines for her from Act V:

we come not to offend,
But with goodwill.

"But, father, isn't that you? Aren't you good will?"
"Right now I am, lovely girl, right now I am."

The next day, when Will went to the shop, Father said to him, "I don't want any more plays read in my house. Lucy still watches me like a hawk."

With that, Gilbert stepped in and looked back at Will. "We need a serious talk about some money Will has brought with him."

Will took out the heavily-laden purse. "Father, I have considered staying here indefinitely. I have brought us more than the schoolmaster earns in three years."

Father looked at the money carefully. "Good for you, but that's not nearly enough. It would take most of this money to set the family right, but then what? Lucy would still be after us, business would still be lousy, and you would have no job."

"But my family wants me to stay."

Father growled, "What would you do to earn a living here?"

Gilbert said, "I've learned a lot about money, so let me put it to you straight. For you to come back to Stratford, you need to bring enough money to buy your own house and invest in farm land to have a yearly income so you don't need to work. At that point, Lucy couldn't touch you."

"Little brother, I'm impressed at your skill. You are quite right."

"Second son always has to work harder."

"I hoped this would be enough to accomplish all that and help Father, but making all that money you're talking about is beyond my reach right now, especially since the playhouses are shut."

"The last news I heard from London is that the plague has lessened. Maybe the playhouses will open again," said Gilbert.

"I think you two are telling me I must leave."

Father said, "Do you see any other choice?"

Will tossed and turned that night. He finally fell asleep, but when he awoke early the next morning, Anne was still asleep. He put his arm around her and she rolled over.

"Are you awake?" He asked.

She rolled half way back. "Now I am."

"I've missed you so much."

She rolled the rest of the way toward him. "I wonder how you feel when you're gone so long."

"My trips home aren't a measure of how much I care."

"Are we closer to getting our own house?"

"No. We'll need a lot more money."

"I know what that means. Do me a favor. Don't make a big fuss about saying goodbye to the children."

"But I don't know how long I'll be gone this time. I'm not sure I can ever make the money we need."

"Will, I have to live with them every day, crowded into this house. Let them cherish happy memories of you reading plays to them, rather than some tearful goodbyes."

After breakfast, Will bid a cheerful adieu to everyone, as if he were just on an errand to Shottery. However, he took the purse with a good portion of the money in it and set out toward London.

Chapter 11

London

Late April 1594

"True is it that we have seen better days."
As You Like It.

James and Helen Burbage lived on Holywell Street in Shoreditch, outside the London walls, because they thought it a safer and cleaner place to raise five children than inside the city. Everyone who lived around them watched out for each other and the children grew up with fine friends. Aside from the occasional thunderous noise of cannons from the nearby Spitalfield artillery yard, it was a quiet neighborhood. Seventeen years earlier, James' brother-in-law financed the building of a playhouse nearby, The Theatre, with a loan backed by his trust. At first, James made a little money in The Theatre from bear-baiting, but when Will's plays started to draw audiences at The Rose, James hoped they might begin to use The Theatre for plays too. The renovations to accommodate plays were almost complete when the plague closed down all public gathering places. The traveling troupe made little money, and James still had to pay a mortgage on the empty playhouse. His eldest son, Cuthbert sold books and worked as a clerk to help keep the family from starving. They all prayed to remain safe from the plague.

Will approached the Burbage house and knocked on their front door repeatedly before it opened.

"By gar, Will Shakespeare, the plague didn't claim you." James gave Will a bear hug. "Come in, come in. Richard will be thrilled to see you're all right."

James' eyes were rimmed by dark circles making Will think he'd been ill. "It's good to be here. I'm eager for news of your family and the plays."

"We've kept our health, thanks be to God, but not our luck." James shouted up the stairs to Richard. "Get down here. There's someone here to collect an old promise."

Richard peered down the stairs and slid down the rail when he saw Will. "All my fears be banished unless you're an apparition."

"Your eyes play no tricks. Here, feel this." Will feigned a blow to Richard's large middle before the two embraced.

"Tell us what you've done," Richard said.

"I've been writing and The Earl of Southampton rewarded my labors handsomely. I'm ready to invest in the troupe."

James grunted. "I welcome your investment, but we have foul circumstances to overcome before there'll be any plays."

"But I wrote one that must be performed in a matter of weeks," Will said. "And what, pray tell, happens then?" Richard asked.

"It hardly matters," James said. "Our patron is dead, the troupe is scattered, and Henslowe won't let us use The Rose any more. The Theatre could be readied soon, but . . ."

"Dead? What happened to Lord Strange?" Will asked.

"He died suddenly last week, soon after he was made Earl of Derby. Rumors fly," Richard said. "Some say he was killed by the same scoundrels who murdered Marlowe."

"We've been completely undone by his death because I can't find another patron." James looked at Will. "What about your Earl?"

"He's barely an adult and is involved in Court intrigue. I've a better idea. You know the Royal Chamberlain, the one in charge of the Queen's entertainment?" Will asked.

"Yes, Lord Hunsdon. We made a few investments together, but he won't help us. All he cares about is his plants and he won't waste his time on things that don't interest him."

"What about the Vice-Chamberlain?" Will said.

"I know him too. The Vice-Chamberlain, Sir Thomas Heneage, is not of high enough standing. You must be at least a baron to sponsor a troupe of actors. I've been through all this."

"Listen to my idea. The Earl's mother, the Countess, will be married to Sir Thomas Heneage soon. At the Earl's urging, I started writing a play in their honor. It's almost completed and we could perform it at their wedding."

"Go on," Richard said.

"If Sir Thomas likes it, maybe he'll persuade the Lord Chamberlain to become our sponsor." Will watched James' face furrow into a frown.

"I don't see how we could assemble the players, get the play finished, get it scribed, make props, and hold rehearsals." James stood up. He started to cough.

"But Father, even that stick-in-the-mud Cuthbert wants the plays started again," Richard said. "Everyone misses being entertained."

"Don't forget your newest investor: me. I need Richard's help to finish the play, then I'll have it scribed and set props and rehearsals. If you can get the troupe together, I guarantee you won't be sorry."

James paced.

"What do we have to lose?" Richard said.

"Money, more money." James paused. "All right, all right we might as well try. But we can't pay anyone until we have a patron, finish The Theatre and attract some audiences."

Richard grabbed Will's arm, and they danced a jig. "Two minutes you're in town and already we're planning our next play. Good Lord, how I've missed you."

"You'll never know what a lifeblood you are to this troupe."

"Get going, you two. We've not a minute to waste," James said. "Wait. What's the play called?"

"A Midsummer's Night's Dream."

"Best not be a nightmare."

Will leaned on the front door to his boarding house and shivered at the cool summer morning. It was too early for anybody to be on the streets. He was tired from two weeks of non-stop work and his patience was thin. Where were James and Richard? He heard the horses before he saw them through the fog. The brothers too had sour looks and no one bothered to say anything as Will climbed into the back of the wagon. It was a quiet journey to Southampton House, where gardeners and servants were frantically running around setting up decorations on the tables and moving chairs for the wedding.

"You see. They aren't any more ready than we are," Richard said.

"Look how many of them there are," Will said.

"Unload this wagon," James said. "I'm going to find the others."

Will tossed a box to Richard. "You're in charge of the fairy dust."

"And who's in charge of the fairies? "At the sound of a familiar voice, Will turned to see the Earl, standing with John Florio, both grinning.

The Earl gave Will a kiss on each cheek. "Is this the famous Richard Burbage?"

Richard put out his hand. "I'm the mortal you honor with the word 'famous'."

"Well-deserved praise," John said. "Your acting talents are well-appreciated."

"I'm eager to see you perform for my mother today." The Earl turned to Will who continued to take props off the wagon.

"I worried you'd stay in Stratford with your family and never come back to London," the Earl said.

"I fancy weddings and couldn't stay away," Will said. "Perhaps yours will be next."

"Don't count on it." The Earl turned to go into the garden. John gave Will a worried look and followed the Earl.

"We've been so busy with this play, you haven't told me about the Earl's place in Titchfield." Richard laughed. "He looks like someone who would make life exciting."

"Censor your thoughts. We've a play to present."

Later that afternoon, the guests entered the courtyard from the flower gardens behind the large house, where the nuptials had taken place. Servants carried trays of light sack and sweetmeats while everyone found their seats. At last, the newly-married couple sat down in front and the head servant nodded to James to start.

Will stood alone with his eyes shut. He was a duke now and was about to be married. What a joyous moment this was. He felt the happiness permeate his body and opened his eyes in time to see James signal. From the stage, he looked at the Countess, radiant from her marital vows and spoke directly to her:

Now, fair Hippolyta, our nuptial hour
Draws on apace: four happy days bring in
Another moon: but, O, methinks how slow
This old moon wanes! she lingers my desires,
Like to a step-dame or a dowager
Long withering out a young man's revenue.

The Countess blushed. Sir Thomas straightened in his chair and took her hand. Although rather elderly, Sir Thomas was still quite handsome. When the Duke was called upon to judge the love wishes of the merchant's daughter, Hermia, Will hoped Sir Thomas would relax and enjoy the story, but it was Puck who moved everyone to laughter when he bungled all the lovers' linkages:

"Lord, what fools these mortals be."

When the rude mechanicals played out their rough version of Pyramus and Thisby, even the servants paused to watch. The play ended with all the lovers content, and there was enough applause to satisfy Will. It worked. He approached the bride and groom and took the Countess's hand. "You have been a most gracious audience, my lady. My congratulations to you both."

"I'm honored by this play you've written for us," The Countess said.

"Well done," Sir Thomas said. "We hope to see more of you now that the playhouses will reopen."

"We're eager to resume, but with the sudden death of Lord Strange, we've lost our patron," Will said.

"He was your sponsor?" Sir Thomas stood. "Untimely death." He put his hand out to his new bride.

"Without a patron, there'll be no more plays from us, your Lordship," Will continued.

Sir Thomas turned back to Will, still holding his bride's hand. "The Lord Chamberlain might sponsor you but he's on the continent right now."

The Countess said, "Perhaps Hippolyta will have a word with him about Rude Mechanicals when he returns."

Chapter 12

London, Dover, Stratford

Late Spring 1596

"When sorrows come, they come not single spies, but in battalions."
Hamlet

Lord Hunsdon came back to England a few weeks later and promptly agreed to sponsor James Burbage's troupe, which now became the Lord Chamberlain's Men. Audiences eager for entertainment after the long plague siege flocked to the Rose and James Burbage's Theatre. Will enjoyed being busy, and rented a room near the Theatre to minimize travel.

One evening, feeling like company, he walked around the corner to the Burbage home. The fresh air felt good after breathing the heavy, black, eye-burning fireplace smoke at his house. The Burbages had servants to air the rooms every day and clean the fine black ash that coated everything. Will's room never had that kind of tending.

Helen Burbage answered his knock. She was a good bit younger than James, and still quite attractive. "You just missed Richard. He thought you would stop by earlier." Helen looked pale and had dark circles under her eyes. "He's hunting in the country now."

"I wanted to see James, too. Is everything all right?"

"Not with James. Come in and see for yourself, but you must be quick as he needs his rest."

Will went into the library where James sat in the dark, feet propped up and eyes half closed.

"James." Will whispered. "Are you awake, or do you watch from your slumber?"

"Sit down close to me. I've felt poorly for a while, but I'm better today."

"What ails you?"

"I had a fever, but it's been chased away by Helen's constant fussing and special medicines."

"A fever is a worry, James."

"At least I have no sores, so it isn't the plague. Besides, I'm too mean to have the sickness come after me. It seeks much sweeter victims. Now, tell me what brings you here."

"Just the usual storytelling. You remember that Marlowe play *The Jew of Malta?* There is a similar plot in a book Richard Field gave me, *Il Pecorone.* I altered the usurious money-lender theme and I think it's a good one."

"That sounds interesting, but I can't think about it now. I've too many problems with playhouses."

"I thought Cuthbert managed The Theatre."

"But I've now become part owner of The Curtain."

"Good. We can use it as an overflow for The Theatre. You'll need this play."

"We may have to quit using The Theatre." James coughed and closed his eyes.

Helen rushed in and applied steaming herbal compresses to his chest. "Talking does this to him," she said.

"I thought news of my new play idea might help, but . . ."

"It's Giles Allen." James sipped some of Helen's brew. "That serpent-faced Puritan remains obstinate about renewing the lease. It expires next year, but he's threatening to cancel sooner."

"That two-faced viper," Will said. "He likes the lease money just fine, but then tells me my plays offend his morals."

"Do you know Blackfriars?" James asked.

"I know it well because Richard Field lives there. It's a large group of buildings that were a Dominican monastery before Henry VIII dissolved them."

"That's the place. Last month in The George, I overheard some gentlemen discuss a difficulty with the sale of a large meeting room in Blackfriars. We could add seats and stage plays indoors all winter."

"Is it larger than Cross Keys?"

"Yes, by far. But, it's costly, £600 initially, and another £250 for carpentry work. But before I commit to this, I must know if I can depend on you to write at least three plays a year."

"That's a lot. There are always new plays kicking around in my head, but I must have time and Richard's help to perfect them."

"I need your plays to attract audiences, and I need assurance I'll get them. This commits every last farthing I can lay my hands on, and I must be certain." James coughed.

Once more, Helen came in with hot compresses and another cup of herbal brew. "Will, I worry about him talking so much."

Will stood up. "Rest and get your strength back. We need you in good health to carry out all these plans."

"Come back in a few days, and we'll plot the money lender story. I'm sure Helen will tell us when I'm strong enough to think and talk at the same time."

"Hope I don't go the way of our patron, Baron Hunsdon."

"What happened?"

"He died of a fever."

"So, we're in trouble again without a sponsor?"

"No, his son is already in place, George Carey, Second Baron of Hunsdon."

"How did that happen so fast?"

"They're cousins of the Queen."

"James, you have too many playhouses and people to worry about. I've plenty of sources, so I'll get started on that money lender play right away."

"What's it called?"

"*The Merchant of Venice*," said Will.

"How soon will it be done?"

"How soon will you be well?"

James continued to have coughing fits that robbed him of his energy. For three months that summer, the troupe went on tour without him, forcing Richard and Will to handle all of James' duties in addition to acting and managing the players.

By August, they had reached the white cliffs of Dover. Will stood at the cliffs and stared across the English Channel as hard as he could in hopes of seeing the French port of Calais. He assumed this was all he would ever see of France. He read about distant lands and spoke with John Florio about his experiences, but the chance of travel to these places was unlikely. Anne didn't even want to go to London. Maybe one day Hamnet would travel with him.

As usual, The Lord Chamberlain's Men hurried through the chore of packing up for their move to the next town. They tore down the makeshift stage they had built in the yard of Maison Dieu Hall. Carefully, they wrapped props and costumes for the jolting wagon journey on rugged country roads. Everything needed to be protected from mud-splattering jolts and the inevitable English rain. The quiet that permeated the group resulted from a dog-tired weariness that sets in after weeks of touring.

Richard pulled hard on a rope that secured the last trunk of costumes. They were the biggest worry because it was important to keep them dry. "So, where to next?"

"Towards home." Will used his sleeve to wipe the sweat off his brow. "I don't know. Somewhere west of here."

"That's a safe direction. We'd get wet if we tried to go east."

"Here Richard, you consult your father's journal. I'm too busy." Will tossed him a roll of foolscap scribbled with names of towns and officials to contact, plays performed in summers past, licensing fees, roadway directions, and names of inns along the way. Entries were crossed out, and the margins were crowded with added notes.

Richard caught the roll, looked at it for a moment and threw it down. "This tour is too long."

Will sat under a tree. "It feels longer, but the days number the same as last summer's. The difference is your father isn't along, directing everything. Be sure to tell him to get well so he can join us next time."

"Maybe that's his sinister way to get us to appreciate his work," Richard said.

"If so, he succeeded. This business of wooing bloated local bailiffs, negotiating licensing fees, performing on crude stages and constantly packing up against the elements and thieves has worn me down."

"You're a bit short, I've noticed."

"And you've lost your great big belly. I'm too weary to even finish my complaint." Will stood up again. "C'mon. Help me cover the trunks."

"If Father can't take care of business in London, we'll have more to do there, too."

"Thanks for the reminder. Now I have nothing to look forward to."

"Why don't you move your family to London?"

"Anne's afraid of London and . . ."

"You could talk her into it, if you wanted."

"She's never left Stratford and the children are . . ."

"I think you like living by yourself."

Will watched the players load their personal belongings onto the wagons. "I can write more plays that way."

They walked slowly across the dusty ground to sit it the shade of the inn.

"Cuthbert says . . ."

"I know he's your elder brother, and you're kind to him, but Cuthbert says a lot of things. What we need is him doing more and saying less," said Will.

"Cuthbert will partake in more of the business if it's required of him. He just doesn't share our fondness for plays."

"He has a fondness for money and that means he has to do more ."

"You'll see. When we get back to London, Father will be fully recovered, Cuthbert will work in the box office, I'll act, and you'll write."

"And the fairies will make us all wealthy and kind. Even Giles Allen."

"Don't leave out the beautiful women who'll fall at my feet, and Ned Alleyn's public admission of my superior acting."

Will laughed. "Ned's out here in the countryside. While we stand here, he saws the air mightily with such grand gestures the clouds part and the winds obey his promethean voice. I see his work in the sky right now."

"We should leave immediately then. He'll make it rain on us."

Will turned toward the road where a dirt-covered rider galloped toward them.

"Good day. I seek the player William Shakespeare."

"I'm William Shakespeare."

"I've a message for you, sir." The rider jumped off and pulled a leather bag from the saddle horn. From that he took a scroll that carried Gilbert's seal.

"My thanks for your troubles." Will handed the rider a coin.

He tore off the seal and read the letter. A message sent like this wouldn't be good news. He read it twice. Hamnet, dear God, not Hamnet. He had to get to Stratford.

Still holding the letter, he grabbed his pack and told Richard. "I have to leave. Hamnet is seriously ill."

Richard put his arm around Will's shoulder. "There's a fast horse in the stable you can take. Go right away."

The messenger added, "I left a good horse in Beaconsfield. He'll be ready for another fast ride by the time you get there. You could exchange yours and make it in three days."

"That I'll do." Will was off without even a glance backward. He thought of Hamnet lying in bed with a fever. He pushed thoughts of Hamnet in a coffin out of his mind. Death. It changed everything.

Usually the sight of the Clopton Bridge on a nice day made Will think of all the times as a youth he and Hamnet Sadler fished under its cooling shadow. Gilbert always tried to tag along and Hamnet usually talked Will into letting him. The bridge was built in 1499 by Sir Hugh Clopton, before Will's father was even born. It set Stratford apart from its neighboring communities by providing a reliable crossing of the Avon River. Today, it marked the end of Will's furious journey home. He spurred his second horse even faster, as if speed would stop anything bad from happening to young Hamnet.

At the familiar house on Henley Street, he jumped off and felt his legs buckle from fatigue. He held tight to the saddle while his legs found their new purpose. Beads of sweat dripped down his face, and his heart thumped so forcefully he could feel it in his chest.

Upstairs, Susanna looked out the window at the sound of a rider. She recognized the form of her father, and ran down the stairs in seconds.

"Daddy, Daddy, Daddy, you're here! You're here!"

Will turned and scooped up his beautiful blond princess at the same moment she jumped into his dirty arms. He gave her a half whirl and a hug before setting her down. She had grown nearly as tall as her mother and had the first face of womanhood.

Susanna stepped backwards. "Oh Daddy, it was awful here. Hamnet just got sick one day and before the week was out, he died. We miss him so much it hurts. We knew you would come quickly, although you smell like you need to wash up before I hug you anymore."

"He's already buried?" Will felt like he'd been struck in the chest. "When?"

"Two days ago."

"I got here as soon as I heard. Be kind and go fetch your mother and sister. Then, bring me some bread and ale."

Will walked around the house to the garden in back and washed in a side bucket with water drawn directly from the well. It was as cold as death. When he turned around, Anne was standing there. Will said "I got here as fast as I could."

She stood there, not moving. "We couldn't wait for you." A tear trickled down her cheek, and Will brushed it away. He put both arms around her thin body and smelled the mixture of flour and smoke in her hair and clothes. She was stiff like his father. Did they both dislike him?

"I'm heartbroken," he said. "I'm sure you did everything you could."

"Your mother and I used herbed cold cloths and boiled hot compresses. Every remedy we could find, but it was no use. The fever was too strong." She looked down. "He asked for you. Your name was in his last breath, but you weren't here."

Will held her chin so he could look into her eyes. She looked away. Then he caught the movement of Judith on the back steps from the kitchen. She still resembled Hamnet, but not as much as before.

"How could I have known?" Will let go of Anne. "I grieve his loss as much as you." He went over to Judith and sat next to her on the step. "Judith, Judith." He put his arms around her. "You've lost your other half."

She buried her head in her father's shoulder and sobbed quietly. They stayed that way for a long time, without a word.

By supper, Will had spoken with everyone except Father. He stayed in the workshop until there was not enough light left to work anymore. When he finally came face to face with Will, he just stared. Will felt the familiar knot inside. "This is a sad day for me. My only son has died."

"If it's so important, how come you're the last to be here?"

"Father…"

"Hush. I don't want to hear your excuses."

That night, Will sat on the bed and ran his hand over the colorful flowers his mother had embroidered on their wedding blanket. "You know I came as fast as I could. I have lost a part of me. I wanted to spend time here with all of you as soon as I had enough money to return for good."

"You've been gone too long. Waiting for you is all we do."

He blew out the candle and got under the blanket. "Is there no end to this? I can't write here."

"I'm forever telling the children you'll return to build us a house. We're tired of waiting."

"I know." Will stared at the darkness and listened to the night sounds. This home was less familiar than his London house. He closed his eyes and saw Hamnet smiling. Behind him was the Dark Lady, also smiling. She had her hand on Hamnet's shoulder.

"You promised me and I believed you," Anne said.

"I meant what I said."

"Meant? But not anymore? You've changed from the person who made that promise when Susanna was born."

"My plays are popular and I make money in London."

"Why don't you just admit you're never coming back because you like it better there."

"I want us to have a family home."

"You'll burn in Hell for your lies to your family."

"My grief lies all within,
And these external manners of lament
Are merely shadows to the unseen grief
That swells with silence in the tortured soul."

"What are you saying?"

"Nothing, Anne, goodnight."

In the days that followed, Will busied himself with the daily affairs of his large family as he had on his last visit. He joined everyone as they worked through the day. In the kitchen, he tended the fire and stirred the pot. Outside, he pulled weeds, picked herbs and flowers, and helped his father whitewash their timbered house. Everyone explained their way through each chore as Will asked them about the simplest task. He continued his fascination with the labors the women pursued with speed and dexterity he never noticed before. He saw how the food preparation for ten people consumed Anne's day as much as the plays consumed his.

Will worked alongside Gilbert in the glover's business he'd abandoned years earlier. How differently the once-familiar tasks struck him now. Sewing looked like a finger dance rather than the painful needle-poking chore of his apprenticeship. Gilbert worked steadily without complaint in a way Will never could. Then Gilbert explained the knowledge required in buying materials and profiting from the finished gloves. He showed Will how they appraised the value of dye and leather. He described the effect of fashion and weather on the quantity of gloves they made each season. Will saw how the glove was a different symbol for each class and occupation. He also saw the business as more complicated than he remembered. In his youth, the familiarity of this scene made it appear uninviting, or maybe he had changed.

In the evenings, Will relaxed with his family as they gathered outside in the garden. In this cool comfort, he listened to their stories of their day and their concerns about life.

One night, after a week at home, he cornered Father when he returned to the workshop to put some things away.

"I enjoyed my work with you this week, but you know Gilbert is a better glover than I ever could have been. It wasn't in my blood."

"You were taught to work hard and earn a living for your family."

"I beg you to forgive my youthful mistakes and let me back in your heart. That was a long time ago. Must I pay for it forever?"

"You ruin people's lives. When your only son cried out for you, his mother had to say you'd be there, but she knew you wouldn't."

"Anne has strengthened our family with her constancy."

"God will make your final judgment, not me. Ask his forgiveness."

"I want your forgiveness."

His father threw some leather scraps into a box. "What do you know about forgiveness? You come and go as you please, knowing full well your mother and wife will always put dinner on the table—dinner that your brother and I earned."

Will gripped the edge of the workbench with trembling hands. "When I was growing up you said forgiveness was part of God's way. You loved being a successful bailiff, why don't you understand that I love being a success at what I do?"

"Your ways are not my ways. I pray to accept this and forgive you. Perhaps one day I will, but not this day."

Later, Will sat on the bed while Anne said her prayers. It had always been like that, and she accepted his unwillingness to pray with her. When she finished, Will took her hand, "I have something to tell you."

Anne looked at him directly, and for a moment, he considered telling her he loved her, but that's not what came out. "I need to go back to

utumn performances are going to start and they need

...y need you? So does your family. Those Londoners care not a whit for you. They just want your plays and the money they earn. But it takes a tragedy to bring you home for a week."

"It will take time. In your prayers, ask God to keep his plagues away from London. I'll work hard to keep my promises."

Anne felt the tears well up in her eyes. "I wonder how much you think about us while you're away. We're stuck in this crowded house with the same chores, household tasks, and the same arguments, while you do whatever you want in London. You never even asked us to join you there."

"That would be impossible. I live simply, in a tiny rented room. You'd hate it there, and be even more upset with me than you are now. Every time I come home, everyone's mad at me. What must I do to show I care?"

"It was Gilbert who went to Hamnet's funeral," Anne said. "You want to know what to do? Stay here. Work here. You care more about your plays than us." Anne rolled over and faced the wall.

"You don't understand. I am my plays. I can't give them up."

Will could see the outline of Anne's back moving slightly with each breath. There was no way she could understand. Was he fair to do this to her? He wrote about people whose weaknesses destroyed the family they loved. Was he one of them? He got up and rubbed his temples. Then he quietly put on his clothes and went out, but not to his usual haunt, the workshop. This time, he went to Hamnet's fresh grave in the churchyard. Will knelt at the wooden cross that marked it.

"Dear Hamnet, so much between you and me is left undone. We should have walked together in our garden while I taught you verses and told you stories. I should have heard your thoughts and discussed your ideas. Instead I was a ghost of a father to you. It's too late to play the most important role of my life for you, but I'll make it up to your sisters. I'll write one play for you and return for them."

At first light, Will packed up his belongings, said farewell to Mother, gave warm hugs to Judith, Susanna, and Anne and rode off for London. No one cried.

Chapter 13

London, Whitehall Palace

1597

> "All the world's a stage,
> And all the men and women merely players;"
> *As You Like It*

In February, James Burbage finally succumbed to the illness that had cruelly ravaged him, and passed away quietly. The troupe, now under Cuthbert's control, barely had time to mourn James' death when they received a royal summons. In March, Queen Elizabeth invited five of the troupe to Whitehall Palace for Lord Hunsdon's official appointment as Lord Chamberlain.

Whitehall Palace had been the English monarch's official residence for more than fifty years, starting with Queen Elizabeth's father, King Henry VIII. Occupying twenty three acres, buildings were built on both sides of King Street, a public thoroughfare. There was a gatehouse connecting the two parts of the palace so the royals never had to go outside.

Now, the appointment day had arrived, and Will, Richard, Cuthbert, Thomas Pope, and the boy actor Robert Goughe stood in a water taxi for the trip to the palace. Will felt stiff and uncomfortable in the doublet he was forced to wear for the occasion. It was left over from before his days at Titchfield and he had gained enough weight since then to make the top too tight for ease of movement. The now out-of-fashion trunk hose and codpiece were replaced with wool Venetian breeches and stockings so his lower half was free, but he dare not spend more for his clothing.

"So, Richard, do you know the story of Whitehall Palace?"

"It's been around longer than I have, so I really don't know. But I'm sure you'll tell me."

"You need to know these things, Richard. Maybe someone will ask, and you don't want to appear stupid."

"I want to hear it," said Robert Goughe.

"Good, here it is. Before 1530, Whitehall was called York Place, town house of the Bishop of York. Cardinal Wolsey built it up to be one of the most impressive residences in London. And Anne Boleyn made her court debut and met King Henry VIII here."

"The King's second wife?" said Cuthbert.

"Quite so. Actually, the King was having an affair with Anne's sister, Mary, and was still married to Catherine of Aragon at the time."

"Evidently, those history books you're always reading get a bit spicy," said Cuthbert.

"The King decided that Anne might be preferable to her sister, but Anne said she would not be any married man's mistress."

"Then what?" said Richard.

"The King charged Cardinal Wolsey to obtain a papal annulment to his marriage to Katherine, so he could marry Anne. The Cardinal failed, and the King punished him by banishment and forfeiture of his possessions."

"So that's how the King obtained the property."

"Right. And, Wolsey being a bachelor, never added apartments for a queen to York Place. When the King visited his new property, his wife didn't accompany him."

"I see. That would make a convenient spot for him to meet Anne Boleyn," said Richard.

"Precisely. Not long after they got their annulment, thanks to Wolsey's successor and a hasty marriage to the King, Anne delivered her first child."

"But, that would be . . . our beloved Queen," said Richard.

"If you're implying that Queen Elizabeth was conceived in what is now Whitehall Palace, you are more of a gossip than I thought," said Cuthbert.

"You know how Will likes to embellish a story," said Richard.

"Gentlemen, I'm just passing along things I read, helping to dispel ignorance."

Just then, they arrived at the waterstairs to Whitehall Palace. They paused near the top of the steps and Cuthbert said, "Look at all that white stone. This is the biggest building I have ever seen."

"Yes, and the buildings and grounds extend across King Street, far to the west. I think this is almost as big as the entire town of Stratford. Come on Robert," said Will, prodding him. "Wait until we see the inside."

Accompanied by palace guards, the five entered, and were led to the Great Hall, where they stood, waiting.

"TRUMPETS, HO! SOUND FORTH!"
"Her Majesty! Her Majesty, the Queen!"

The guards stamped and ushers bowed as Queen Elizabeth walked toward her throne. Her ramrod straight posture and deliberate pace were impressive. She wore a gown of royal blue satin trimmed with pearls and sapphires. A triple layered ruff of lace and linen framed the Queen's face, while a crown and jewels adorned her royal head. Her attendant ladies followed, their eyes downcast, and everyone bowed or curtsied as she passed. They all played their parts as well as the best actors.

Queen Elizabeth walked up the steps to the platform that raised her throne above everyone while her attendants took their places at her side. Two lords approached and spoke briefly with her before she called forth another to discuss affairs of the day. All bowed and scraped in her presence.

One of the lords walked off the podium and brought George Carey, Lord Hunsdon, from the audience. He knelt before the Queen, head bowed. Finally, the aging Sir William Cecil, Lord Burghley, first minister to the Queen, stood at her side with a large rolled parchment.

He removed the wax seal and unrolled it with both hands before announcing:

"Her Royal Majesty, Queen Elizabeth, Queen of England, with the agreement of her Lords of Council and for the good of all England, on this day, names George Carey, Lord Hunsdon, to the Privy Council as Lord Chamberlain."

The Queen leaned forward to tie a velvet robe on their kneeling patron, "Lord Hunsdon, I hereby declare you the new Lord Chamberlain. George, my cousin, your father served me with great distinction, and I have every reason to believe you will do likewise, as long as you remember who is in charge here."

"Your Majesty, it is a great honor to serve you."

The Queen smiled. "The better you understand me, the better you will serve me, George. I am told some of your players have accompanied you here today."

"Indeed so, Your Majesty. They do me great honor, and I pray they have your favor as well."

"Oh, be assured, I look forward to their plays every time they're scheduled. Their performances at Christmastime were our pleasure. Pray have them step forward, that I might have a word with them."

She spoke first to the shortest and heaviest of the four. "You must be Richard Burbage, the masterful player of Richard III. No one will forget, *'A horse, a horse. My kingdom for a horse!'*"

Richard colored slightly. "I am flattered by your recognition and praise, Your Highness. It's great sport to play at villainy."

"I expect to see you play other roles. After all, England doesn't want to be known only for its villains. We have great fools and lovers, too. Who are these other gentlemen with you?"

"This is my brother, Cuthbert, our playwright, William Shakespeare and my fellow actor, Robert Goughe."

They all bowed deeply.

Queen Elizabeth turned first to Cuthbert. "I see a strong family resemblance. Are you a businessman like your father?"

"I am, Your Majesty."

"I was sorry to hear of his untimely death. He has undoubtedly gone to his great reward, joining my cousin, George's father. I'm sure you will make your father's memory proud with your management of the troupe."

The Queen then looked at Will. "Master Shakespeare, you put the best words in the mouths of these players. I thought of one of your creations the other day. There was some controversy about Falstaff and the prior Lord Chamberlain, Oldcastle or something, but I've forgotten the detail of it. That's what happens when you become old. You forget the awkward things."

"When the old Lord Hunsdon was Chamberlain, he always said that the Queen only forgot that which was not worth remembering," Will said.

"That sounds like something that old flatterer would have said. Now, tell me, what further plans do you have for this character, Falstaff?"

"He'll probably die honorably in the next history play, Your Highness, in some way that would befit an old soldier."

"Oh, I think it would be most unkind to see him slip away without some romantic interest. I'm often amused by the cowardly actions of soldiers in the presence of women."

The Queen glanced around the room and noted the general mirth at her suggestion. "You see, Master Shakespeare? That would make a great play idea. Falstaff in love. What say you to that?"

"Indeed, it's a wonderful idea. He shall start falling in love before we leave this room, Your Highness," Will said.

"Very good, Master Shakespeare." The Queen turned to their patron. "George, have your players ready with this new play for the Order of the Garter Feast on April 23rd. You've prided yourself on your speed and this is your chance to be quick for my sake."

"Your Majesty, I cannot promise for the players . . ."

Will stepped forward. "Your Majesty shall not be disappointed. Such a man as Falstaff has a huge capacity for love, particularly if his Queen wishes it."

Cuthbert and Richard glanced at each other.

"Good. You have barely a fortnight, so I hold you excused, as I know you must be about your business." The Queen waved them off with a flick of her wrist.

It was over. The Lord Chamberlain's Men bowed deeply as they retreated.

As soon as they were out of the Great Hall, Richard exploded. "God shield us, Will, what did you tell the Queen that for? There are no books about Falstaff. How can you make up a story so quickly?"

Will tried to reach up to put a hand on Richard's shoulder, but his doublet wouldn't let him. "The Queen tests our patron. If the guests are poorly entertained, he'll be the butt of their jokes, not us."

"But we're the ones who face the audience and our future at court."

Will laughed. "Calm yourself, Richard. I'm writing this play as we walk. Tomorrow, go about town and find three scribes who will hold their time open for us by week's end. Then we'll have almost a week for rehearsal."

"Master Perfect will write this in one week?" Cuthbert said.

"My promise."

"Well, it better be good," Cuthbert said. "We have problems with Giles Allen and maybe the Queen will order him to renew our ground lease."

Will stopped. "Suppose he perseveres in this absurd position. Where else can we stage our plays?"

"Nowhere. The other playhouses are small and not available. I offered Giles Allen £ 24 a year, £ 10 more than the previous lease. His answer was he'd think about it." Cuthbert sounded discouraged. "His next letter said there was some new clause he wanted to add, but wasn't ready to discuss it yet. Of course, we still have precedence at the Curtain."

Richard wrinkled his nose. "I hate the Curtain. It's too small, and they can never get the smell of the bear baitings out."

"Last time we were there, I was covered with flea bites," Will said.

"What about that playhouse space your father purchased at Blackfriars?"

"Our patron was one of the Blackfriars' residents who petitioned the Privy Council last year to ban public performances there," Cuthbert said. "They didn't want unsavory players or theater-goers in their neighborhood. Maybe now is the time to ask him when Blackfriars will be available for plays."

Richard said, "Let me understand this. After next week, we have no place to rehearse a play which is not yet written that the Queen expects us to perform in less than two weeks."

"I think I'd better start right now," Will said. "Find someone to play my part today, and bring me some supper."

They watched him run down the street toward home, arms at his sides. They laughed at his awkward gait before they took off themselves.

All that week, Will saw Richard once a day when he brought food from home or the tavern and they went over lines together. For this play, Will chose the familiar setting of Windsor. He searched out his scribbled notes for scenes that were never used, ones that had special appeal to audiences, and ideas he had jotted down for future use. Reading through these notes jogged his mind and he was able to pen a rough draft within three days. For two more days he added details and lines. Not once did he look at the unfinished play *Hamlet*.

The scribes started copying exactly five days after the meeting with the Queen, and soon they had three clean copies ready for the players. On the first day of rehearsal, Giles Allen stopped at The Theatre, but someone warned Cuthbert ahead of time and he ducked out the back.

On the second day, Giles Allen returned. He was a thin and wiry man with close-set eyes and wore a tall hat of the type usually favored by Puritans. This time, he caught Cuthbert by surprise. "Your lease is up. Clear out your things."

"Let's not be hasty about this." Cuthbert gestured toward the benches that lined the first row of the lower gallery. "Let's talk." He allowed Giles Allen to take the lead. They climbed two steps and suddenly Cuthbert fell to the floor, moaning. All play rehearsal stopped and the entire cast gathered around them.

"What happened?" Richard asked.

"Master Allen pushed him." Will Kempe offered.

"I did not, you lying agents of the devil," Giles Allen said.

Cuthbert moaned. "My leg."

"Lie still and we'll wrap it," Richard said.

Giles Allen began to move away. The players surrounded him. "What have you done to Cuthbert?"

"We should do the same to you."

"It's not my fault he fell," Giles Allen said.

"I saw you push him."

"I'll call the constable," Augustine Phillips said.

Giles Allen looked around at the players. "You lying ruffians. Deliver £20 to my room at The George by this evening. You can continue until Christmastime. Then no more of you on my land."

"After we take care of Cuthbert," Richard said.

The players moved aside to let Giles Allen leave.

Will leaned over Cuthbert. "I never knew you could act."

"Only when I'm negotiating a contract." Cuthbert stood up and bowed. The players applauded.

Six days that week, they rehearsed in the morning, presented regularly scheduled plays in the afternoon and spent evenings at home or in The George. There were few complaints about their schedule because everyone knew this performance could end their troupe if the Queen was dissatisfied. Finally, they were ready.

The Great Hall at Whitehall Palace didn't have a tiring house, so the players and backstage helpers changed costumes and readied props in a small area behind scenery screens. Richard Burbage wore extra padding under his waistcoat to transform his figure from ample to round. He scowled at fellow players who bumped into him as they moved about their crowded tiring area. Richard disliked his Falstaff costume for *The Merry Wives of Windsor,* but tonight's audience made the inconvenience worth his effort. They were the most influential members of England's society, gathered to honor those newly inducted into the highest order of knighthood in the world, the Knights of the Garter.

Richard reached out and grabbed Will when he walked past. "You seem calm tonight. How can you be certain this grand audience will take kindly to such a simple play?"

Will was outfitted in his own clothes for his part as the country Justice Shallow. "This audience is like the royalty in our history plays. Their favorite person is always the fool. Besides, laughter will make them feel good and they'll enjoy the play. You should try it sometime. It might improve your mood."

"All those nobles make me anxious. It's a good thing you didn't double me in this play. I couldn't make a costume change fast enough."

Will poked Richard's padding. "You are doubled."

"But the playwright isn't." Richard smiled grudgingly. "Tell me how you wrote this play so fast. I must know your secret in case the Queen asks."

Will adopted Justice Shallow's pedantic voice. "Almost all of it is written in blank verse, which flows quickly from the pen. Poetry requires more invention, thus more time. Also, the French Doctor Caius and the Welsh schoolmaster Evans speak fractured English. It's easy to write and the foreigners will like it."

"I see your method. The groundlings will like it, too."

"With some alterations," Will said. "No one else would understand the part about the Germans who didn't pay their bill."

"I don't understand it," Richard said.

"You should have asked. Count Mompelgart, one of the inductees tonight, left England last time without paying his bills. He pestered the Queen for five years to become a Knight of the Garter, and now he can't attend the ceremony this evening without being arrested."

Richard laughed. "What a name. You should make him one of your characters. Where did you get the character Justice Shallow? How well he is named."

"A fellow a lot like him chased me out of Stratford." Will laughed. "I really should go back and thank him, but I think this is enough gratitude."

"The Queen is ready," Lord Hunsdon said. "You must bow to her at the end."

"Yes, yes. We know."

Will was first on stage and he was completely relaxed. Tonight, his part put him on stage once in each act except the last. He watched the Queen's reaction as much as he could. She laughed occasionally, but kept her face passive much of the time. Maybe she wasn't enjoying it. When the play ended, the new Lord Chamberlain walked onto the stage.

The players followed and all bowed to the Queen. She began to clap and the other guests joined her.

"George, several of my counsellors pointed out how difficult it must be to write and stage a play in only a fortnight, yet your players accomplished it rather well." She looked directly at Will. "Master Shakespeare, you must be a driven fellow. You responded well to my challenge, with just one exception."

Will looked at her. Uh oh, Will thought. Here it comes.

"Master Shakespeare, my charge was to show Falstaff in love, yet he never actually became amorous with any of the women in the play."

The room was quiet. "Your Majesty's keen observational powers may have noticed that the character Pistol alluded to that matter in the last act, when he said,

'Our radiant Queen hates sluts and sluttery.'"

Queen Elizabeth laughed. "I'm entertained by your subtlety, Master Shakespeare. I look forward to seeing more of your plays here."

The success of this play would finally give Will freedom to work on *Hamlet* while the troupe presented old plays and he had time off from acting.

Chapter 14

Stratford

Early 1597

"I like this place and willingly could waste my time in it"
As You Like It

Gilbert Shakespeare stood in front of the former site of Hamnet Sadler's bakery on Sheep Street. Charred remains of the building were cruel reminders of the fire that almost ruined Hamnet completely. He worked hard to rebuild, but the new structure would only be about a quarter the size of the original.

Hamnet said, "How are Anne and the children? You are such a loyal brother and friend to remain in Stratford for them."

"They're as good as can be expected, but you know how difficult it is when a child dies."

"Oh, yes. But, Gilbert, don't you miss all the travel and contacts from your haberdasher years?"

"A little, but dragging along all the cloth, hides, needles, thread, and such grew tiresome after the first year. It was interesting at times, but Stratford remains my home. Better to be a baker like you with all those delicious aromas."

"That was true for quite a long time, but then the fire . . ."

"At least, you are rebuilding."

"It's a slow process. Fire relief hasn't been much of a help, what with all the other fires here."

"I know Stratford had a series of disasters while I traveled."

"There have been too many for Fire Relief to be much help to me. There's been a drought for two years now."

"I see how low the Avon is. . ."

"Between the weather, the fires, and the plague, it's been strange here for a while. Why, just the other day I heard an odd story."

"Do tell."

"Remember William Underhill? He was a few years older than us, but lived in that big house on Chapel Lane."

"Yes, the old Clopton house, oddly called New Place, but it is hardly new."

"That's the one. It seems that William has been sick, and the house and grounds haven't been tended for a while. Now he wants to sell the place for a bargain price before the overgrowth catches fire and he loses everything. That would be an ideal house for my large brood and bakery, but I've got no money."

"Now that you mention the Underhills, they had some family connection with a haberdasher I called on in Idlicote. One of William's sons visited there once, telling wild stories about fights between his older brother Fulke and his father. I thought it was just a teenager's imagination, but family can be difficult when there's lots of money involved."

"Speaking of family, isn't your sister Joan about to get married?"

"Yes, she and William Hart have it all set up for this summer. Maybe I should tell him about the house, or even Will. He's got to come back sooner or later and he promised Anne to buy a house."

"How about you, Gilbert? Is marriage in your future?"

Gilbert laughed. "I leave that to the rest of my family. Now I must get home, but I'll come by to help you rebuild whenever I have time."

Gilbert said his goodbyes and let Hamnet return to his work. On his way home, he walked past the house called New Place and tried to envision its interior. Maybe it would be good for Anne and Will.

Gilbert spent the next week making some discreet inquiries, sending messages to London, negotiating, and signing papers. Then he walked into the kitchen of the Henley Street house.

"Anne, could you spare an hour or so to go for a walk with me?"

Anne looked to Mother, who nodded, and said, "I suppose, but where?"

"You'll see."

Gilbert and Anne walked the four blocks to Chapel Street, and stopped in front of New Place.

Gilbert pointed at the house and said, "What do you think of this house?"

"It's badly overgrown, looks like it needs some work, but I see a huge house with ten chimneys, five handsome gables and two barns. This is the old Clopton house, isn't it?"

"Not any more. Now, it's yours."

"Gilbert, is this some cruel joke?"

"I have the papers right here. This house was for sale, and I bought it on behalf of Will, who sent the money. Now, it's yours."

Anne took a step back, then almost knocked Gilbert down when she threw her arms around him and gave him a big kiss on the lips. "I can't believe it." Her eyes filled with tears.

"Come, look inside." They walked into every room, opening doors and talking about the possibilities for cleaning it up. "This place is even bigger than it looks from the outside. It does need lots of work, but it's huge. Oh, Gilbert, I want to begin right away, getting it into shape. I'll start right here in the kitchen." She looked around at the neglect. "It can stand lots of cleaning."

"I'll be happy to help."

Anne gave Gilbert a funny look he'd never seen before. "Gilbert, you've done so much already. It's not suitable for the girls to live here yet, but if I moved in, we could get a lot done quickly. Would you mind staying here with me? This is so big and scary…"

"Yes. The girls wouldn't be much help but I would thoroughly enjoy staying here with you." This time, Gilbert leaned in with a tender kiss.

They exchanged a long look, then Gilbert said, "Anne, I…"

"Hush," she said. She grabbed his arm and pulled him toward the stairway. "There's a bed upstairs that must be tested."

Chapter 15

London; The Theatre

Winter 1597

> "Blow, blow, thou winter wind!
> Thou art not so unkind as man's ingratitude."
> *As You Like It*

For the next eighteen months, The Lord Chamberlain's Men had to perform every play at The Curtain because The Theatre ground lease remained unresolved and Giles Allen refused to let them inside the building. Even though Will and Richard rehearsed and planned new plays every day from first light to last, they didn't earn much because The Curtain was half the size of The Theatre. Will worried that he had overextended himself by purchasing New Place. His father had done the very same thing when he reached the pinnacle of his success. He'd bought the house next door and doubled the size of their living area as well as creating a workshop for his glove business. That renovation required him to connect the two houses with usable living space. It had proven to be more expensive than he'd estimated and that one mistake had ruined him. He would never again have the money or spirit to succeed.

Will's troupe put on extra performances, which helped pay for the renovation at New Place, but allowed little time for visits to Stratford. He left all the house decisions to Anne and Gilbert.

Early one morning, the players were rehearsing an old play, when a shout rang out from the back of The Curtain.

"Rogue! THIEF! I'll get the fellows on your back for stealing. OVER HERE," cried a stage boy.

Richard screamed, "Quiet, you whoreson, insolent noise-maker! We must get this scene right, and there can be no more interruptions. What is it now, Sincler?"

"A thousand pardons, Richard, but I saw movement by the door and found this fellow outside, listening."

Sincler held the cape of a squarely built man with a scraggly beard and a very prominent nose, who stood there smoothing out the creases in his rumpled garments as he glowered at Richard. "I did not spy. I simply waited for a convenient time to announce my presence."

"Your presence is duly noted. Now, state your purpose and be quick about it," Richard said. "We have work to do."

"Brevity will not be the issue when you see my writing. My name is Benjamin Jonson, and I'm here to present my play to you."

"Well, I'm Richard Burbage, and it's customary to hear plays in the tavern after dark."

"I break the custom for a more private hearing."

"Wait a minute, I know you. Haven't you played with Ned Alleyn at The Rose?" Richard said.

"Indeed, I had that dubious honor."

"Well, Master Jonson, since you play for our biggest rival, why should I not have you beaten as a churlish spy?"

"It's not as it might appear, Master Burbage, or else I wouldn't have been so forthright with my name. Unfortunate circumstances conspired to force this approach."

Richard's face reddened. "Listen, you busy meddling fiend, I haven't a moment for you right now. Come back another time. Now, be off before I have you arrested."

Will stepped onto the stage from the tiring house. "Wait a moment, Richard. Continue your rehearsal. I'll look at Master Jonson's play."

"As you wish. I have no time to argue." Richard turned abruptly.

Ben waited until Will was within speaking distance. "Are you William Shakespeare?"

"Quite so. Just call me Will."

"You're most generous to look at my play."

"We always want new plays. Even if they arrive oddly-cloaked." Will looked over the short, portly man whose rumpled, torn clothes made him look more like a beggar than a playmaker.

Ben squirmed. "I heard you started as a player."

"My station was even lower. I did anything to earn a farthing. I painted scenery, polished swords, and straightened candles." Will smiled. "Now I paint word pictures, polish phrases, and straighten actors. What theatre experience do you claim?"

"I too, started as a player," Ben said. "Then I mended plays for Philip Henslowe so he could fatten up his own coffers."

"Are you one of the culprits who served a prison term for that *Isle of Dogs* disaster?"

"Most unfortunately. Then Henslowe didn't trust me to write any more, even though everyone knows the affair was Nashe's fault."

"Have you shown this play to Henslowe?"

"I tried, but he won't even look at it. He says I'm too old and difficult for him."

"How old are you?"

"Twenty-six."

"I was twenty-six when James Burbage took a chance with my first play. Besides, if Henslowe and Alleyn don't want it, we probably do. What's it about?"

"Fools. I call it *Every Man in His Humour.*"

"Good. Comedies play well, and every man likes to see the other man the fool. Read me a sample."

With that cue, Ben Jonson lowered his head and leaned forward. Then he slowly raised his round upper body, cocked his head to one side and fixed his gaze on Will:

> *"Well penned: I would fain see all the Poets of our time pen such another play as that was; they'll prate and swagger, and keep a stir of art and devices, when (by God's so) they are the most shallow, pitiful fellows that live upon the face of the earth again."*

Will laughed. "What's the name of this character who insults poets?"

"Bobadilla," Ben said. "His humour is that of a braggart and a coward. Other characters have different humours, and I play them against each other."

"Tell me about the others."

"I have one man for every humour. Each tries to achieve beyond anything reasonable, thus shows himself a fool. There is Prospero, Doctor Clement, Peto, Piso, Cob and his wife, Tib."

"Interesting names to go with your humours. I'll read the play tonight and discuss it with you tomorrow."

"Your company would do well with this solid comedy in the classic style. My words are oft quoted in London and my characters good enough to be used as lessons on children's behavior. You'll fill The Curtain with this play."

"I trust you don't include modesty among your personal humours. Come by tomorrow after supper. Now I must go." Will turned.

"You'll need £ 2 to secure this play," Ben said.

"Tomorrow," Will said.

In the next few weeks, The Lord Chamberlain's Men presented several new plays at The Curtain, among them Ben Jonson's *Every Man in His Humour*. One afternoon, John Florio saw it and sought out Will afterwards at The George.

Will embraced his old friend. "You're a good sight for these weary eyes. Sit down with me. We work so hard these days I haven't any leisure time."

John raised his glass to Will. "In Italian, I'd call you Benvolio, Good Will. Now a toast to Italians. May their humours entertain us in England."

Will raised his glass. "Ben Jonson's play will humour us all for a long time. You know, I suggested he write about Englishmen, but Ben is hardly receptive to suggestions. He drinks here so I'll make sure you meet him."

"He uses words and ideas in clever ways, but he doesn't have your gift," John said. "Your words are like pleasing musical notes to a master composer."

"I'm honored by your flattery. Ben's fickle humours often make him sour. He's a difficult fellow."

"Which reminds me of our Earl," John said.

"Wait, Ben is walking this way." Will stood up and waved. "Over here. Meet a friend of mine who admires your play, Master John Florio."

"Greetings," Ben said. "This makes you my friend as well."

"I'm jealous to be surrounded by gentlemen so blessed with the gift of words," John said. "Show me again how your character Thorello speaks of his jealousy."

Ben Jonson puffed up his burly chest and blurted:

'For this I find, where jealousy is fed,
Horns in the mind are worse than horns in the head.
See what a drove of horns fly in the air,
Wing'd with my cleansed and my credulous breath:
Watch them, suspicious eyes, watch where they fall,
See, see, on heads that think they have none at all.

Ben bowed to the nearby patrons who banged their flagons of ale on the heavy oak tables and cheered his performance.

John moved closer to Ben. "Italian men are famous for jealousies, but what about the ones closer to home. I'd love to see foolish Englishmen in a play."

"Fools know no boundaries. I set this play far from England in order to appease the Master of the Revels. Look though he did, he found no English politics in my play." Ben looked smug. "I also stayed true to the classical form to satisfy other critics."

"We sold every seat, so you did the right thing," Will said. "Make sure you show me your next play before Henslowe sees it."

"I shall. Now, please allow me to leave. I see someone who has avoided me and I shall seize this opportunity to confront him while he's off guard."

John watched Ben. "A rough man, don't you think? Too much for our Earl."

"Odd fellows buzz around the playhouses like flies around honey. Place House at Titchfield had its share, too."

John laughed. "But not enough for you, eh? I miss you. The Earl does, too. Now he's in over his head again. He was introduced at court to Elizabeth Vernon by her cousin, the Earl of Essex . . ."

"I can see it now, another woman. Pretty young thing?"

"You know our Harry. Whenever he came to London, they'd share every moment. While in Paris last month with Essex -some shady business for the court- he got an urgent message from her."

"With child?"

John nodded. "He came straight home and married her."

Will laughed. "Not the kind of wedding the Countess had in mind when she nagged him to settle down."

"It's not as funny as it might be." John waited as a barmaid passed. "Elizabeth Vernon is a lady-in-waiting to the Queen and Her Royal Highness wasn't amused. She's threatening to send them both to The Tower."

Will gulped his ale. "Since when does the Queen use The Tower to punish lovers? Who told you this?"

"They violated her consent rule, which she took as a slap in the face."

"They don't belong in the Tower," Will said.

"I'm only telling you this because he may ask for your help." John leaned close. "Stay away, Will. Don't touch it with a barge pole."

"The Queen likes my plays. Maybe I could flatter her into a less harsh punishment."

"You'd get squashed like a flea. The Earl has protection from a higher station than ours." John dug into his pouch and produced the second page of a letter. "From Robert Cecil to his cousin Francis Bacon."

I knew she would send them both to the Tower, and I implored her to be merciful to the young Earl. I reminded her that as a ward of my father after the Earl's own father died, he was like a brother to me. I swore that I would watch him carefully and make sure he served her well, if only she would not send him to The Tower. I am painfully aware of the difficulty of this promise because the Earl has such an unpredictable nature, but he must learn to bring it under control. Further, the more I can keep him away from that insolent Earl of Essex, the better. Their friendship is a grave concern to me and I will do whatever I must to keep them apart.

I would be most grateful for anything you can do to help me in this endeavor. Father would certainly expect me to continue our protection of the Earl, and I must honor his memory, no matter how difficult.

Written this day the 2nd of October 1598.
With Kindest Regards, Robert Cecil xx
Secretary of State

Will handed the letter back. "How did you get this?"

"I show you this to keep you from interfering," John said.

"But..."

"Now, I bring exciting news." John pulled a blue leather-bound book from his bag. "At long last, my dictionary is published."

Will opened it eagerly. "*The Worlde of Words.* What a treasure. This calls for a celebration." Will raised his goblet. "To success and truth."

"To words. How many of them have we exchanged over the years."

"Ah," Will said. "Our truest friends." Then he leaned closer and whispered to John. "Tell me how you possess a letter from Robert Cecil."

"This must remain our secret." John glanced around, then drank slowly. "Fifty years ago, my father worked for Robert Cecil's father, William, as a minister and Italian tutor. I spent much of my youth at the Cecil estate. Now we tell each other about matters of mutual interest."

Will drummed his fingers on the table as he stared into the eyes of his friend. "So, that's why the Earl regards you as a big brother. It's almost like my brother Edmund and me."

A loud commotion at the other end of the tavern drew their attention. Ben Jonson shouted. "You lying, insulting cheat, Gabriel

Spencer. I accept your challenge. Meet me at Finsbury Fields at first light tomorrow." He turned and left quickly.

Will stood. "Fools! Some find trouble with women of the court, others court trouble as if she were a woman. John, I'd best try to catch Ben before he gets arrested for dueling."

"You meddle too much in the affairs of others."

"We need his plays."

Will found Ben outside. "I can't rescue you from foolish decisions, but I can remind you of the obligations to your wife and children."

"The only way I can achieve peace of mind is to keep my honor," Ben said.

Will thought of his father's twisted sense of honor and how he never learned from his mistakes. "You're too wise a man to defeat yourself in wars of your own making." Will turned and left.

A month after the duel, Will and Ben met again. This time, they were outside The Theatre and it was the middle of the coldest night of the year.

Will was trying to move a huge support beam that lay on the ground. He was sweating in spite of the cold, and cursing under his breath. When Ben walked up to him, Will stood, so they were face to face. "Remove yourself, unless you're here to help us."

Ben shook his head. "I couldn't sleep and went out for a walk."

Will thrust a torch into his hands. "Then hold this, so I can use both hands."

Will stooped over the wooden beam and painted a number on it.

"Aren't you worried someone will come and arrest you?" Ben said.

"If you're worried, move along, but keep quiet."

Richard and three of the players dragged up a sled and started loading beams on it.

"What in God's sweet name are you doing?" Ben said.

"I said quiet. And hold that torch higher."

Will reached for the end of the nearest beam to get a feel for its weight. "You have a bit of the gossip in you. That's the problem with a reputation. We can't risk it's true."

Ben handed the torch to one of the boys standing by. "I won't say a thing about this. I owe you that much. But I best not hang around. Whatever you're doing, if it gets me arrested, only the Queen could save me."

"Try chatting up the nearest constable and walk him away from the river. Then you can help us without seeming to. And Ben," Will leaned toward him. "Giles Allen's ownership of the land doesn't include the playhouse that sits on it, any more than Shylock's pound of flesh included any of Antonio's blood."

Ben laughed. "I didn't see a thing, Mistress Portia." He clapped Will on the shoulder and walked away.

James Burbage's old friend, carpenter Peter Street staggered by, dragging one end of a beam. "Someone we know?" he asked.

"No one to worry about," Will said. "Everything look all right to you?"

"It's going well." He put down the beam. "I'll help with the next wall so it won't come crashing down like that other one did." Then he led some men around to the west wall, where they climbed to the roof and attached ropes with hooks.

"Lower it slowly," Peter Street said.

This time the noise was not as loud and the group quickly loaded the oak beams onto large sleds. Will and four others pushed the first sled downhill toward the frozen Thames. Their grunts were suddenly replaced with curses when the sled hit a patch of ice and for a moment careened away from them. It stopped at the edge of the riverbank, and they ran down to push it again. This time it slid smoothly onto the ice, and out a good ten paces. They whispered a cheer and ran after it.

In the middle of the river, a single loud crack bounced from bank to bank. The men stood frozen, not even daring an oath.

"Come on," Will whispered after a few moments. "Lighter loads next time."

They pushed the sled the rest of the way across to vacant land in Southwark, where vagrants huddled around a fire.

"A penny each to help us," Will called out. He showed them where to drag and unload the sled, then crossed the river with his men for the next load.

By the time the last of The Theatre was down on the ground and every beam marked and ready to be moved, Will and Richard had crossed the Thames twice. Meanwhile, a few people had gathered to watch.

"Richard," Will said, "Get into your constable's uniform." Will continued to load beams, and a few minutes later, he heard Richard's voice amongst the crowd.

"No loitering here, you're in the way. Be off with you."

"But this is Giles Allen's," one of them said. "What are you doing at this hour of the night?"

Richard the constable raised his club. "Official business. Be off with you or you'll taste this." The neighbors backed off, cursing. "You haven't heard the last of this."

By first light, all the timber had been moved across the Thames to Southwark, with only small bits of broken wattle and daub left on Giles Allen's land. Plus, of course, potential lawsuits.

Chapter 16

London

1599

"Now is the winter of our discontent."
King Richard III

Building The Globe from the Theatre remains filled most of Will's time during the first six months of 1599. The Burbages retained a part interest in the Curtain, but Cuthbert overruled Will's idea of staging extra plays there while the Globe was built.

"I want to make 'em hungry for our plays," Cuthbert said.

"I'm the one who's hungry," Will said. "My family is stuck with a half-finished home."

"The more work you do on The Globe, the sooner it'll be open," Cuthbert said.

"I'm a writer, not a carpenter. Tell me what happened with Giles Allen after we tore down The Theatre."

Cuthbert chuckled. "Oh, he was beside himself. But, now the matter is in the courts. That's where I work best. All the delays I can think of just buys us time to build The Globe. Once we're done, no court will make us take it down. How about what you do best? Do you have any new plays?"

"I have a wonderful one almost done. It's one I've worked on for a long time."

"When the Globe is finished, you can quit acting completely and just write plays, but we need you here until we're actually making money," Cuthbert said.

"I plan to hold you to that promise," Will said.

Will worked harder than ever to finish The Globe. He was the first one there in the morning and the last to leave at night. Every night he stayed up late writing by candlelight. When the other players complained about doing carpentry work all day, he encouraged them with tales of new plays and more money. Finally, the Globe opened and the audiences came. Will was either at the playhouse filling in for drunk or sick players or home writing more plays.

During all this, the play that consumed most of Will's attention was *The Tragedy of Hamlet, Prince of Denmark*. Richard would play the role of Hamlet, dressed in dark fitted clothing. Will would be the ghost of Hamlet's father, dressed in silver breast plate and armor, with a wig and white powder in his hair. Will was eager for the play to go on since he'd added scenes and altered others. They'd never actually rehearsed the whole play, but he knew it was a good story.

Opening day was dark and foreboding.

"It's going to rain," Richard said. "This play seems too long. I thought you were going to shorten it,"

"You're just being crabby," answered Will. "It's too late to cut now."

"Rain will turn your powder to putty, and we'll have a ghostly comedy," Richard said.

"I hear your cue, Richard. Be a prince and go on stage."

Will listened to the tale of King Claudius, Queen Gertrude and Prince Hamlet in one part of his mind while he searched for places to cut the story in another. He couldn't let any of it go. Soon, it was his turn on stage in conversation with Richard.

"Whither wilt thou lead me? Speak; I'll go no further."
"Mark me."
"I will."
"My hour is almost come,
When I to sulf'rous and tormenting flames

Must render up myself."

They both lost themselves in their roles. The audience hung on every word uttered by the ghost:

"Adieu, adieu, adieu. Remember me."

Will exited the stage and hurried through the tiring house. The trap door that covered the stairway below was open for him. He ran down the steps into the darkness under stage center. Curtained against prying eyes, this little room was completely dark. The damp air and the smell of wet dirt made it seem even smaller. Will began to sweat as he listened for his cue lines. Then, in a deep and ghostly voice, he said,

Swear.

Richard answered and Will continued:

Swear by his sword.

Richard answered again. Will got hotter. Hamlet, Hamnet, Hamnet, Hamlet. Will saw Hamnet in his coffin. He spoke his last line:

Swear.

Will could hardly breathe. He scrambled out of the tiny room and up the stairs where he sat on the tiring house floor, soaked in perspiration.

"Are you all right?" Richard leaned down for a closer look.

"It's too tight down there. Maybe Goughe should do it. He's small enough."

"No, his voice isn't right."

"Someone . . ."

"We'll decide later. Did you figure out where to cut it?" Richard said.

"I don't know. I'll see how you handle the long speeches."

"That's where you should cut. They're too long, and no one will listen."

"Impossible. Those are the best parts," shouted Will.

"Quiet!" the tiring house master said.

Will listened as Rosencrantz and Guildenstern met the new King. Why did John Florio demand he use those names? They didn't sound Danish. But John had been right about so many other things. . .

Richard went back on stage:

"To be or not to be; that is the question;
Whether 'tis nobler in the mind to suffer
The slings and arrows of outrageous fortune,
Or to take arms against a sea of troubles,
And by opposing end them. . . . "

Will walked over to where he could see the audience better. Then he heard the thunder. He still hadn't figured out where to make cuts.

Later in the play, Hamlet addressed the players for the play-within-a-play:

"Speak the speech, I pray you, as I pronounced it to
you, trippingly on the tongue. But if you mouth it as many
of our players do, I had as lief the town crier spoke my
lines. Nor do not saw the air too much with your hand,
thus..."

More thunder. The groundlings yelled. "End it, end it."

Will grabbed a roll and began marking out lines and whole scenes. Henry Condell took the completed changes and tacked them on a wooden post. The actors went to work studying them. Finally, the duel scene started, and so did the rain. It wasn't enough to bother at first, but became a downpour by the time everyone lay dead on the stage. That opening night, Horatio and Fortinbras never spoke their final lines.

Will stood to one side of the tiring house as the players rushed to get out of soaked clothes. Richard peeled off his shoes and poured water from them onto the floor. "Even those cuts weren't enough."

Cuthbert said, "This will never do. We'll lose our audiences unless you fix it, and quickly."

"I won't change a word. This is my best play." Will snatched up his cape and left. The rain pounded in his dilemma. As he walked, the sight of Anne's tears and his father scolding him flashed through his mind. He hadn't cried since that day four years ago when he stood over Hamnet's grave. Unlike the play, Hamnet was the ghost and Will was the one alive. He needed more than a play to honor him. He needed to return to Stratford.

Chapter 17

London; St. Paul's Cathedral

Early 1601

"Cry "Havoc," and let slip the dogs of war."
Julius Caesar

St. Paul's was the scene of many unusual happenings, but this one was quite rare. Two Earls, dressed in ordinary clothes, sat in the middle of the huge church, with no one anywhere near them. They spoke in low voices.

"Robert, what forces this secret meeting?" said the Earl of Southampton.

"You know how Sir Stink undermined me with the Queen while we were in Ireland?" said the Earl of Essex. "I need your help at court."

"Ever since your cousin Elizabeth and I married, you know the Queen finds me a troublemaker, so I'm unwelcome at court. Besides, we have two young daughters at home now. I must protect them."

"I know, I know. But it's gotten more serious. You know my monopoly on sweet wines?"

"I think of you collecting on every bottle as I drink my fill." Southampton laughed.

"It's not funny anymore, Harry. Sir Stink convinced Robert Cecil, the Queen's hunchback secretary of state, to not renew my monopoly because our Ireland campaign wasn't as successful as he wanted."

"That's terrible. Without that income, things don't look so rosy for you."

"What's more, Cecil's spies watch my every move. I need your help, but I don't want to get you into trouble."

"About all I do any more is go to plays and drink your sweet wine. I'm badly in the Queen's disfavor. How could I possibly help?"

"I need a favor with Robert Cecil."

"I knew him well in my youth. When my father died, I became a ward of his father, William Cecil, and he and I shared tutors. But that was years ago, and I've seen little of him since."

"But, if you could get him to renew my control over sweet wine . . ."

"I'm sure the Queen would see right through that, Robert."

"I'm grasping at straws here, Harry. I've had to reinforce my defenses at Essex House, in case Sir Stink tries to assassinate me."

"Can't you just appeal to the Queen yourself, directly? You were once her favorite."

"That still rankles with Sir Stink. His men would keep me out of the palace. This whole affair reeks of corruption at the highest level. They want to ruin me. I'm a war hero, but Raleigh has that tobacco company in the colonies. Money talks."

"I saw a play once about a dishonest King. Richard II wouldn't give Henry Bolingbroke his lands back and Bolingbroke had to confront him with force of arms."

"Harry, if worse comes to worst, that may be what I have to do. Since you know all those players, if I send you a message about plays, have them present it. Was it Richard II?"

"Yes, that's the one. But it's hardly played any more, they have many newer, more popular plays."

"Make it a special request. Send our friends from the Irish campaign to request it, and I'll pay to have them buy half the seats if they have to. I'll send my men, so they can see what could happen to a corrupt monarch."

In early February, Essex sent the message. Southampton rounded up six mutual friends and sent them to the Globe to speak to the Lord Chamberlain's Men. Although the players were initially reluctant, forty shillings convinced them it was a good idea, and they played it on Saturday, February 7. The audience was mostly Essex sympathizers, but the ever-present spies also attended, and reported to Robert Cecil before the day ended.

Robert Cecil succeeded his father, William Cecil as Queen Elizabeth's secretary of state. She nicknamed him "my little pygmy" because he suffered acute spinal curvature. That didn't stop him from approaching the queen with anything he thought important. He told her, "Your majesty, it has come to our attention that many of the Earl of Essex's friends attended a little-seen play earlier today."

"Good, I hope plays will keep them out of trouble."

"That might not be the case, majesty. Lord Chamberlain's Men presented Shakespeare's Richard II. No one has seen that old chestnut for years. Do you recall it? Richard II refuses to give seized lands back to Bolingbroke, and he deposes the King."

"Good heavens. I am Richard II, know you not that? Send Thomas Egerton and several others to Essex House tomorrow to summon him here. We'll have it out with him, once and for all."

Early the next day, four messengers showed up at Essex House.

"The Queen demands your presence immediately."

Essex felt a wave of panic. He desperately wanted an audience with the Queen to explain his grievances, but not under these conditions. "Indeed, she shall have my presence. Please wait in my library while I prepare."

Once inside, the library doors were locked from the outside. "Men, our plan to see the Queen today has lost the element of surprise but we'll go anyway, and enlist like-minded citizens along the way. There will be so many of us she'll have to see us on our terms."

Essex's followers, some 200 strong who had gathered outside according to his earlier plan, set out from Essex House toward London proper

Wearing ordinary clothing rather than armor, Essex still cut a dashing figure with his size and military bearing. "First, we must link up with the Sheriff of London. He promised he could get 1000 men to join our cause. Meanwhile, talk to everyone you see about our grievances."

"Yes, sir."

The group surged forward, chanting "Murder, Murder, God Save the Queen!" "For the Queen, For the Queen!" "The Queen's evil councilors want to sell England to Spain!"

When they arrived at the Sheriff's house, without any formalities, Essex asked, "Can you deliver?"

"Of course, but speed is of the essence. I'll meet you at Ludgate with as many as I can round up."

"Wonderful. We'll get plenty more, then march on down to Whitehall. There'll be so many of us the Queen will have to see us."

Suddenly, an even louder clamor arose outside. Essex's aide approached. "Sir, Robert Cecil's brother Thomas and several heralds are proclaiming you as a traitor. We drove them away, but not before the herald's message was heard."

"This could be my undoing." Essex walked outside and saw people closing their doors, hastening away from the streets. He heard one man say, "Don't want this kind of trouble." Those who had recently joined his band began to melt away.

Essex motioned to his followers. "Quick, men. Let's hurry to Ludgate to meet the Sheriff's men, and we'll return to Essex House to regroup." Perhaps the hostages there might help his cause.

As they approached Ludgate, they noticed a large blockade had been erected. "Can we get through?"

"Not without a fight, sir. It appears to be well manned."

"How about another gate, then?"

"We have reports that all city gates are locked."

He had to get back to Essex House to think about what to do next. "Wait here until I send word." Essex hastened to the river by himself and boarded a water taxi that took him to Essex House.

Once inside, he went to the library, only to find the door open and the Queen's councilors gone. "What happened here?" He could feel his heart racing.

"Sir Ferdinand Gorges took responsibility. He said things might get much worse if they were thought to be prisoners, and he left with them for Whitehall."

"He might well be correct." Essex began gathering papers and throwing them into the fireplace.

Before long, an emissary of the Earl of Nottingham arrived with a stern message: "You are surrounded, and there is a cannon aimed at your front door. Surrender, or else." It was over.

Essex was dragged off to the Tower. In the brief but ugly trial that followed, Essex was found guilty, along with the Earl of Southampton and several others. Prosecutors also summoned Augustin Phllips, the Chamberlain's Men's business manager to explain the troupe's presentation of Richard II just before the Earl's plot played out.

Will had no idea that his old play had any significance any more. He was still brooding about *Hamlet*.

Chapter 18

Stratford

Autumn 1601

"We have heard the chimes at midnight."
Henry IV Part 2

John Shakespeare was dead. Black fabric covered the windows, doors, stairs and even the mirrors of the Shakespeare home on Henley Street. All of the Shakespeare family mourned together except Will. They received guests in the front room, where the heavy oak casket stood. Gilbert looked out the window, hoping to see some sign of Will.

Holy Trinity's vicar, John Rogers, took his place at the head of the casket. He held a black prayer book with both hands and looked about the room in a silent command for everyone's attention. When he cleared his throat loudly, they hushed. He read a brief common prayer for the dead, then placed the first of the evergreen sprigs on the plain coffin lid. Every mourner added his own sprig in tribute. Mother took the first sip from the communal wine vessel while Susanna made sure that each child received a small coin. Finally, the male mourners tied branches of rosemary to their hats. With all the traditional rituals complete, the downcast group silently filed outside to begin the sorrowful march to lay their friend to rest.

The great bells of Holy Trinity Church began their slow melancholy peal. The coffin, now buried in the evergreens of eternity, was placed in

117

a horse-drawn wagon. A black canopy was unfurled over it, and the procession started its slow march. Just as they arrived at the church, a coach pulled up, and Will emerged, sweating. He immediately joined the pallbearers and they carried the coffin from the wagon. With the coffin now inside the church, Will moved to the first pew to join his family. He gave Mother a warm hug, and nodded to the others in order to not interrupt the service. There would be time for them soon enough. Vicar Rogers opened his prayer book and began to read the familiar words.

After the service ended, the family and friends made the familiar walk home to share thoughts and feelings about Father while they ate special cakes prepared by Hamnet Sadler and drank ale.

When the last of the mourners departed, Will said to Mother, "Father was a good man and lived a long and productive life. We'll all miss him."

"I know you two didn't always get along, but he loved you dearly and wanted the best for you."

"Perhaps our love for each other was not a traditional one, but it was real and strong. Now we have to make sure you are cared for. Edmund . . ." he hugged his younger brother, "you are a fine young man, and I'm sure you'll assist with Richard. Joan has her own family and Gilbert is helping Anne with New Place so your support for Mother is absolutely necessary."

Mother said, "Don't worry about me, Will. I'll be fine. But what about you? When are you coming back?"

"I would love to say soon, but there is a lot going on in London. I'll do the best I can."

"I hope you will; you always try. But don't work yourself to death like your father did."

Gilbert walked into the room and said quietly, "John Combe says he must speak with us before you leave Stratford. I assume you won't be here long, so I told him we'd be over after the service."

The Combe house was the only one in Stratford larger than New Place. It had been a Catholic College until Henry VIII seized it for the crown. Will had never been inside, even though John had served on the town council with Father twenty-six years earlier. It was with some curiosity that Will now entered the dark and well-stocked library.

John Combe greeted Will and Gilbert. He was a tall, thin man with a beard that was snow-white but neatly trimmed. "Come in and sit down. You'll have to tend to yourselves as I've let go many of the servants and am not in the best of health myself. I'll get right to the point. Your father and I had some business dealings through the years and I assume he didn't tell you about them. He liked to keep his secrets." John Combe fidgeted with the blanket on his knees. "But there were some things I thought you'd want to know, especially if you intend to stay in this town. In the early years, when your father was making quite a nice bit of money, it was not all because of glove-making."

"I've been gloving and wool-dealing for twenty years," Gilbert said. "I never could figure how he made so much money during those times. He refused to tell me any of the details"

"It happened like this. The gloves were actually part of his money-lending business. If a man borrowed £10, then he also bought a 5 shilling pair of gloves for £2 cash . . ."

"And that would comply with the law, because no interest was charged," Gilbert said. "But later, the borrower had to pay back the full £10."

"Exactly. Except it could lead to trouble. I warned your father that he better be careful about who he made those loans to."

"And I suppose Father didn't listen," Will said.

"For a long time, it didn't matter, but difficulties in your family resulted in most of his borrowers returning the gloves with only part of the borrowed money. He collected no interest, but everyone knew he couldn't go to court because the loan interest charges were not allowed by law."

"So, he was lending free money," Gilbert said. "But why didn't they pay all they owed?"

"People are strange about money." John sat up straighter and looked at Gilbert. "They get spooked over some silly superstition and lose confidence."

"Or see a chance to get something for nothing because of someone else's misfortune," Will said.

"What do you mean?" Gilbert looked at Will.

"That Christmas when Richard kicked Archbishop Whitgrift embarrassed Father in front of the whole church," Will said. "Father had carried our sister Anne out of the church because of her coughing attack. I said something to Mother, and Richard escaped while she was distracted. I take the fault to be mine."

"No one knew that Richard didn't talk?" Gilbert asked. "I don't remember that."

Will looked at Gilbert. "No one really knew Richard, and they blamed Father for his odd behavior."

"It was a most unfortunate affair," John Combe said. "Before that incident, your father anticipated that he would continue to collect high interest, so he borrowed additional money from his friends. That way, he could lend even more to others. He had a lot of money on loan, and to make matters worse, some of the borrowers succumbed to the plague, so many loans were never repaid."

"Then the money his borrowers returned wasn't enough to pay back what Father had borrowed." Will shook his head.

"Who did he borrow from?" Gilbert asked.

"Several of us. We served on the Town Council with him, and we knew he'd be good for the money. He paid most of us back slowly, over many years. Sometimes he'd put money in a little leather bag with his mark on it. Then he'd hang it from our front door early in the morning, before he thought anyone was awake."

"So he still owes you?" Gilbert asked.

"Yes. I suppose he figured I could wait easier than others, so I was the last. Now that he's gone, I thought you should know."

"Does anyone else know about this?" Will asked.

"They're all dead now, except me. It's money my heirs should inherit."

"How much did he still owe you?" Will asked.

"Another £ 88."

"Father left us with nothing," said Will.

"I'm not surprised. I'm sure he paid me whatever he could. He was an honorable man."

"Master Combe, we appreciate knowing this, but we are in no position to do anything about it right now," said Will.

"You gentlemen do whatever you think is right. I wanted you to know so my heirs could not make the story worse. I trust you will honor the debt as best you can. I would show you out, but moving is too difficult for me. Good day."

On the way out, Will and Gilbert looked at the ground in front of them, but no words were exchanged. Their thoughts were about Father and his constant anger.

When they arrived at New Place, Will said, "Anne, I'm sorry about being late."

"Do you mean today or the last several years?"

"Anne... You know Father never made me feel welcome in Stratford."

"I'm sorry. That came out way worse than I intended it to be. Your Father was difficult to live with for me, too. I know you've been busy in London..."

"Busy doesn't even begin to explain my travails. Besides writing plays, which isn't easy, our troupe tore down one playhouse, built another, have been fending off lawsuits, and were summoned by the Queen because of a plot against the Crown,..."

Gilbert said, "A plot against the Queen? Are you in trouble?"

"Not us. The Earl of Essex was executed, and my friend the Earl of Southampton was spared execution, but thrown in the Tower."

"What about the troupe? Can you still present plays?"

"Oh, yes. As John Florio pointed out, we're players, not plotters. John says the same person who got Southampton's sentence commuted excused us. Besides, the Queen likes us since we wrote *The Merry Wives of Windsor* for her."

Susanna said, "*In love the heavens themselves do guide the state. Money buys lands, and wives are sold by fate.*"

"That's from Act V. How did you know that quote?"

"Uncle Gilbert got several pieces of your plays."

"Yes, but how can you read them?"

Gilbert said, "Not all the money you send home goes for food and your new house, Will. Susanna was so jealous of my reading your letters that I taught her some, then hired a tutor." Gilbert and Susanna both smiled. Will turned and hugged them. "We've got some money to talk about, soon."

Judith began to sob quietly. "What's wrong, honey?" said Anne.

"I'm just so sad that Hamnet never got to see our house."

"We'll just have to enjoy it not only for ourselves, but for him. Keep his memory in your thoughts, just as I do," said Will.

Will looked around at the partially finished rooms. "It looks grand here, but much remains to be done." The kitchen looked best of all, so they settled there to talk.

"Gilbert, we were close to following our plan to use the money I send home, but after today, we're a good bit short. I've brought more money to help with the house makeover, and there might be even more soon. Once we've paid off John Combe, I want you to look for land investment opportunities to generate some yearly income."

Just then, the door burst open, and Edmund walked in, breathless. "Will, I've got to talk to you alone." Edmund was the tallest of the brothers, quite handsome, and with a shock of unruly black hair. He always seemed to carry a sense of urgency about him.

"I'm listening."

"Father would never approve of it, but now that he's gone, I want to come to London and become a player like you."

"I'm flattered, but…"

"I'm twenty-one now, so I'm free to do as I like."

"Yes, but do you want to leave Mother home alone with Richard?"

"Well, no, but…"

"London is a rough place, and things are too unsettled right now for me to find you a good spot. How about you stay here for at least another year. I'll get things lined up properly, and we can have a brotherly good time."

Edmund looked pensive, then said,,"Does that mean you'll be there a while? I could stay here another year, but I'll hold you to that promise." He turned on his heel and left. Someone had finally listened to him.

"There's still more to talk about, Will," said Gilbert.

"Of course. But I've had a long coach ride and a difficult day. I'm exhausted."

"I understand. It's just . . ."

"Besides, I'm eager to share my bed with my wife." He moved toward Anne and put his arm around her waist. "Go stay at Henley Street with Mother and come back first thing tomorrow. I'll leave just after breakfast, so we'll have a little time. And Gilbert, I must commend your help. Without your support, our family would fall apart. Isn't that so, Anne?" Anne nodded. "Girls?"

"We love Uncle Gilbert, Daddy," said Susanna. "He's always here when we need him."

Anne just smiled, looked at Gilbert and then looked down at the floor lest anyone see her blush.

Chapter 19

London

!603

> "Fair is foul, and foul is fair."
> *Macbeth*

Criers throughout London spread the news: "The Queen is dead, long live the King." Londoners gathered to await the arrival of her body from Richmond Palace and pray for her soul. Although her health had been failing for some time, her death was still a shock. Queen Elizabeth's demise also signaled the end of the Lord Chamberlain's patron, and hence the protection enjoyed by Will's troupe.

Will worried about his future with the new king, and knew his only antidote to worry was to write. He picked up the worn copy of Holinshed and thumbed through the thick pages. He knew every story in it. This book had spurred his mind and brought him more wealth than he ever thought possible, but now he needed something new. He put it down and picked up Ovid's *Metamorphosis*. Maybe his inspiration would be in here. He opened the shutters and sat down at the writing table, but not much morning sunlight penetrated. The window was too small to let in enough light for writing. Perhaps this was a sign he was not meant to write more. He closed his eyes for a moment and was interrupted by the distinctive rap of John Florio.

"Just in time to help me unpack. How did you ever find me here?" Will said.

"I know where my friends are." John looked around. "What made you leave Southwark?"

"It's quieter here."

John reached for a pile of books on a chair he aimed to sit on. "Where do you want these?"

"Out the window would probably be best. I won't need them if the plays never start up again."

"You've made it through other closings and you'll make it through this one." John put the books on the one shelf in the room. "King James just arrived. Are you writing something to celebrate?"

"I'm rewriting *Love's Labors Won* and changing its name. Queen Elizabeth hated it, you know."

"Do you save all your old plays?"

"Only the ones I think I'll use again. I spend most of my time writing something new."

John put the last books on a dusty chest. "You should hire someone to clean here."

"I send all my money home."

John smiled. "Suppose I tell you your money worries are over, thanks to Rosencrantz and Guildenstern."

"Those two? I thought Hamlet took care of them."

"Here." John handed Will a letter. "Robert Cecil wrote this to his cousin, Francis Bacon. A copy was transcribed for me."

Will read:

At last, with almost all the particulars worked out, James VI of Scotland is fully ready to become James I of England. He acknowledged the burial and monument plans for Queen Elizabeth to the last detail, as she anticipated he would. The King claims that England is so much larger and richer than Scotland, he can do anything he chooses. I respectfully pointed out that the Privy Council keeps a watchful eye on the treasury and sets limits. He assented to this, but I do not think he believed me.

Before we could complete plans for the orderly succession, King James asked me who were London's finest players. It took me so by surprise, I could not think. The King simply repeated his question, louder. For the life of me, all I could recall was that story John Florio told me about how he had his friend name two characters Rosencrantz and Guildenstern. They were relatives of that Danish astronomer Tycho Brahe, who had an observatory on an island off the coast of Denmark. When James went to marry Anne, a storm forced them to spend some time on Tycho's island and they became quite friendly. So, I told James about Shakespeare's characters and he was amazed.

With no further ado, the King motioned to one of his people, and said, "This Shakespeare fellow must be quite good. Have Lawrence Fletcher contact him." Then he said to me, "Fletcher knows the kind of plays we like. Whatever the usual rate has been, we shall double it, and the players shall be called 'The King's Men.' Queen Anne will have her own players, but they will not be as good as mine." At this, he laughed, and farted loudly. This way of conducting the affairs of court departs from our usual custom, but perhaps we will find a way to benefit from such change.

Will looked up. "Us? Double pay! The new King's barely here, and you already have me installed as his royal playwright? You're amazing."

"I also know that our new Queen's passion for language requires the services of a highly-respected Italian tutor."

Will managed a smile. "Once more we serve the upper crust just what they need - words."

"I now command that the King's play maker and the Queen's Italian tutor have a small celebration, or do you still feel duty-bound to finish here?" John asked.

"I don't know what to think anymore." Will dug around in his cabinets and found a crusty pitcher of sack and two glasses. He blew off the dust and poured stout measures for them both.

They toasted their new positions heartily.

"John, it still amazes me that you know so much and so many people far above my station, yet you remain kind to me."

John laughed. "I knew all about you before we even met. We both love words, perhaps more than the people that say them. But Will, there's more to this news about the King," John said. "James is no Elizabeth."

"She could be difficult..."

"You must be prepared to meet a king unlike any monarch you ever imagined."

Will drank his sack. "The double pay should do much to prepare me."

"I hope it's enough."

That night, Will put aside his favorite books and started to think about a celebration play, but no ideas took shape. In desperation, he went through his old plays and resurrected one that he thought would please the new monarch, *Twelfth Night*.

A month later, Will was back at Whitehall Palace. He watched as servants walked in, arms loaded with firewood, cushions and trays of food. Their dress was more relaxed than Queen Elizabeth's servants with fewer frills and looser doublets, but still quite elegant. When they spoke, Will strained to understand their words. He looked around for someone he knew from Queen Elizabeth's reign, but it appeared that everyone was new and of Scottish descent. Will moved toward their make-shift scenery when a skinny little man with a scraggly beard ran up to him and bowed. "Pardon, good man. Somethin' aught be got for you? Abide by me, at your service."

Will thought about his meaning. "Are you asking if I might need some help?"

"That Ah am, Master Burge, that Ah am. Ah couldn't ken the likes of you, but decided you had the face and the shoes of an actor."

"True, but I haven't the face or the shoes of Master Burbage, that's for certain."

"Well, then, point him out to me as Ah tire of this lookin' for naught. The King'll want a report and Ah 'ave to be tellin' him something for it."

"You can find him over there." Will pointed in Richard's direction. "Come on, I'll take you over to him."

The little man walked on his toes and stayed behind so that Will had to keep turning around to make sure he still followed. Hopefully, Richard hadn't spied their approach, for he was certain to greet them with a cutting remark.

Richard sat on a chair eating a piece of fruit he had grabbed from one of the trays being carried to the buffet at the end of the Hall. He ate even more than before to relieve his anxiety since his marriage two years earlier. Now he didn't need pillows to play Falstaff.

"I have a messenger from King James who is eager to meet you," Will said.

The man bowed again. "Yes, yes. Ah've looked about this hall all over for you and now here you are. Can something be got fr you? Here at my service to King James."

"Well, have you a name, before I send you anywhere?" Richard said.

"Ah am Ian Bruce at your service. Somethin' aught be got fr you?"

"We need wig powder and black leggings for a fellow about my size." Richard stood up so Ian could see that although Richard was round, he was not a tall man. "Now be quick before the King comes and wants his play started."

Will laughed as Ian Bruce tip-toed quickly toward the door.

"I don't think I've ever met anyone quite like him, even in one of your plays," Richard said.

"Now I can't wait to meet our new King," Will said.

"From what I've seen so far, it might be questionable who is entertaining whom in this room."

Time dragged. The players began to gather around Will and Richard. Bored by the wait, Will Sly took out a deck of cards and dealt hands of Primero. As Will paced, he kept his eyes on the main entry doors hoping to catch an early glimpse of the royal entourage.

Presently, Ian Bruce returned empty-handed.

"Where's my wig powder?" said Richard.

"No pig chowder here. Somethin' else?"

"Oh, come o'er my ear and repeat your sweet sound," Richard said.

Ian stepped back and looked around. "Beggar. Are you the same man that sent me for pig chowder?"

"Wig powder! How will your King judge me with too little powder, my man?"

"'e will tell you how 'e feels. Ah cannot speak for 'im."

"Is he not predictable?"

"To some. 'e likes to please the Queen."

Suddenly, everyone fell silent. A large group of formally dressed people burst through the main doors, chattering to each other. Then forty royal trumpeters took their places on either side of the long carpet that was stretched the length of the room. They played their fanfare and the herald shouted:

"THEIR ROYAL MAJESTIES,
KING JAMES AND QUEEN ANNE,
MOST ROYAL HIGHNESSES AND MAJESTIES OF ALL ENGLAND AND SCOTLAND"

King James made his appearance without pause. He was not a tall man, and had spindly legs that left him with an awkward gait. He appeared larger due to bulky padding to protect him from assassins. He leaned on servants for support and showed his impatience, as if this evening's entertainment was an inconvenience to be gotten over quickly. He kept his eyes on the throne at the end of the hall and leaned heavily on a gold sceptre too large for his small frame. A heavily jeweled crown rested on his ears and covered his eyebrows. Queen Anne walked behind him, nodding to her subjects as each bowed or curtsied with her passing. She wore a fine brocade gown with full triple ruff at the neck, but no amount of finery could detract from her large hooked nose and pointed features. Will watched them climb the raised platform and sit on their gold-braided thrones.

The Lord Chamberlain stepped forward and bowed. "Your Royal Majesties, I am honored to present the comedy called *Twelfth Night* by William Shakespeare."

"Ay, Ay," King James said. "Get oan wi' it." His thick Scottish brogue tumbled from a small mouth that made him sound as if his tongue was swollen.

Two musicians strolled on stage, playing lutes, followed by a group of Lords, including Richard Burbage as the love-sick Duke of Ilyria:

If music be the food of love, play on;
Give me excess of it, that, surfeiting,
The appetite may sicken, and so die.

Will kept his eyes on the King who looked around the room and fidgeted with the trim on his royal robes. Queen Anne sat to his right with a smile frozen on her face. They were not drawn to the performers. On stage, as ship captain, Will spoke directly to the King as often as possible, but nothing seemed to hold his attention. Off stage, Will paced. Every other performance of *Twelfth Night* had pleased the audience.

When Thomas Pope played Olivia's ne'er-do-well uncle, Sir Toby Belch, King James said. "Guid idea, brin' me some sack." With that, the audience came alive and laughed at Malvolio. As soon as Richard Cowley staggered forth as the drunken friend, Sir Andrew Aguecheek, Queen Anne clapped her hands together and said something unintelligible to one of her ladies-in-waiting. Two stood up and danced in a circle. Then four servants appeared with goblets and four more with pitchers of sack as the members of court mimicked the play. When Andrew Aguecheek danced to the music of the lute, the Queen stood up again and danced along. The players paced their lines, just as they did for unruly groundlings.

When Sir Toby Belch said:

Dost thou think,
because thou art virtuous,
there shall be no more cakes and ale?

The King said, "Tell tha' daft Puritan there will be plenty of cakes and ale. Brin' oan th' food and drink."

Soon, dozens of servants with food trays and pitchers of ale or sack walked between players and audience. They even offered food to the players who had no problem swigging the ale.

The troupe continued, trying to use the commotion to their benefit. As the drinking increased, so did the remarks, and the players adlibbed to make it more fun.

Malvolio read the letter sent to trap him:

"...but be not afraid of greatness. Some are born great, some achieve greatness, and others have greatness thrust upon 'em."

The King yelled, "An' Ah've got aw three."

The player Augustin Phillips said, "That's why you're King and I'm Malvolio."

Toward the end, as all the confused identities were sorted out, Malvolio made his final angry remarks:

"I'll be revenged on the whole pack of you."

But King James laughed at him and the others followed suit.

Then Robert Armin, in his part as Feste, the clown, started the final song,

A great while ago, the world begun,...

But no one could hear him, so he walked out amongst the audience, singing. By sheer persistent repetition, everyone, even the King and Queen, joined in:

With hey, ho, the wind and the rain,
But that's all one, our play is done,
And we'll strive to please you every day.

At last, the players took their bows and King James once more became the focus of attention. "That was quite tidy. Noo Ah want to know who is Master Shakespeare"

Still in his sea captain costume, Will stepped forward and bowed. King James squinted, "'Neath that captain's clothing must lie a clever lad. Tell me, who does Malvolio represent?"

"He resembles no one person, your Majesty. His name is the opposite of a character from an earlier play, Benvolio."

"Naw. Ah was sure Malvolio sits on my privy council." There was nervous laughter in the room. "Now, Ah want to see this other lad, Benvolio. What play was he in?"

"*Romeo and Juliet*, your Highness."

"Guid. Make 'at yer next performance."

Queen Anne said, "Wait. Is there more singing and dancing in *Romer and Julius?*"

"The Queen likes those things written by Ben Jonson and . . . what's his name?" One of the nearby lords whispered to the King. "Oh, yes. Inigo Jones and Master Jonson are writing a masque. It will be filled with gay dancing, just to please her. But from you, Master Shakespeare, Ah want something a wee bit different. Give me a play that takes place in Scotland."

"Your majesty's wish is my command. A play in Scotland will be next."

"I heard you have one about my Denmark," Queen Anne said. "I want that one first."

"Well, then, that's the way we'll have it. Save your Scottish play till later," King James said. "Wha' is this play about Denmark called?"

"*The Tragedy of Hamlet, Prince of Denmark,* It's a fine play and you won't be disappointed.

"Ah've heard of it. It has the lads Rosencrantz and Guildenstern," King James said.

Will nodded.

"Ah met their grandson on an island, on mah way to pick up my lovely Queen." The King chuckled. "Make sure it has dancing in it for the Queen."

The King stood up, adjusted his codpiece with a loud sigh and farted. At his signal, one of his attendants walked over to help him down the steps. The King smiled and put his arms around the attendant's neck. The two of them walked awkwardly toward the door, both smiling broadly.

"Richard, isn't that your friend Ian Bruce?"

"I thought he was your friend."

The King, Queen, and the remaining sixty members of the entourage walked out of the room slowly, chatting as if no one else was there.

Richard and Will moved as fast as they could to pack up their things and leave. "I think they liked it," Will said.

Richard put his arm around Will's shoulders in the same way James often had. "Our new King is quite a fellow, isn't he? I hear he bathes once a year, whether he needs it or not."

"I never thought I'd miss Elizabeth's ways."

"We haven't a choice in these matters. If we're all finished here, I must be off. Winifred still mourns the death of our Frances and frets constantly about our other daughter becoming ill."

"You're good to comfort her," Will said. He tried to imagine going right home to Anne after a performance, but no picture formed in his mind. They watched a wagon pull away, loaded with props and costumes. "I feel a headache starting. I think I'll go home."

"Looks like we need a Scotland play, don't you agree?" Richard asked.

"One with plenty of music, too." Will groaned.

Chapter 20

Stratford, then London

1607

"The miserable have no other medicine but only hope."
Measure for Measure

Standing in front of the mirror, Anne Shakespeare made one more pull on the piece of fabric that flared out at her hip, then gave up. It would have to do. The boned bodice dug into her ribs, but she knew it made her look good. She had spent the hours since sunup with Will's mother and the girls while servants laced them into farthingales and rolls before putting on the layered petticoats that made their dresses full and fashionable. They laughed and yanked, until, with final tugs from their servant girl, Liddy, they finally made it into their garments. Then they twirled around and admired how the fine clothes changed them. Mary Shakespeare confided to Anne that she found the dresses almost unbearable, but the marriage of Susanna to John Hall made the discomfort worthwhile.

That morning, activity at New Place quickened from first light as the servants cleaned, polished and tidied. The house never looked so good. Outside, intense red petunias and blue hollyhocks provided soothing background to the frenzy inside. Wonderful smells of savory meats and cakes wafted through the house while musicians tuning their instruments competed with servants shouting orders.

Will grabbed John Hall's arm the minute he walked in the door. "Join me for a few moments in the library. I've been told not to touch my books today, but no one said I couldn't talk." Will smoothed the front of his fine linen doublet decorated with sashes. His starched ruff scratched his neck even though it was made by the finest London tailors from the sheerest linen.

"Wonderful idea. Staying out of the way seems like the best plan."

They shut the library door, and Will gestured for John to sit on one of the red leather chairs in front of his desk, while he sat behind it. John was quite tall and handsome, with a dark beard and mustache.

"I'm pleased you and Susanna intend to live so close." He leaned back in his chair.

"Susanna was insistent that we buy Hall's Croft as soon as she heard it was to be sold. I had an inheritance from my father.who accumulated some wealth as the only doctor in Bedfordshire so there was no problem making the purchase."

"You've chosen both your house and a fine woman to make it a home for she is well suited to be wife and daughter at the same time. Her mother gets the credit for bringing her up. I neglected the children while I spent so much time in London."

"You've more than made up for your absence by . . ."

"I often wonder. I cannot forget that Susanna's brother Hamnet died before he ever saw any of my plays."

"That's difficult. My father and I were very close.

"After today, I guess you'll know the women in our family are strong and the men have their hands full."

"That's what I liked most about Susanna." John looked directly at Will. "You made sure she could read and write. I cannot abide women who act like glorified servants or princesses."

"Her uncle Gilbert deserves most of the credit for that."

Just then, Judith knocked and opened the door.

"Here you are. I knew you'd run off to your favorite spot. You waste no time in teaching John your ways. Mother wants you downstairs soon, as the guests arrive on the hour."

"Tell your mother I'll appear at my appointed spot, and nothing will keep this eager groom from his chosen place."

When she left, John turned to Will. "I pray Susanna and I fill our home with the same spirit you've filled this one."

"I hope you fill your house with more than spirits. Grandfather is a part I desire to play." Will rested his elbows on the desk. "My Grandfather Arden, who died before I was born, had eight daughters and no sons. He never let them forget their children would have Arden blood, even without the Arden name. Now Susanna has that same legacy."

John smiled. "Indeed, our children will know they carry Arden and Shakespeare blood. Naming them may be a difficult problem, but one we face with joy."

"Naming characters is one of the most interesting parts of play writing." Will rubbed his temples. "In your practice, are you able to relieve pain?"

"I try to find ways, especially in the stomach. Many people think doctors heal them, but I believe doctors simply help the body heal itself."

There was another knock and the door opened. Edmund Shakespeare, looking tired and road-worn, walked in. "Greetings, I'm much later than I was supposed to be, I know." He looked at Will, ignoring John. "I need to see you right away, before the wedding."

"You do see me, and you also see Susanna's bridegroom, John Hall."

John stood and offered his hand to Edmund. "You must be Susanna's uncle who also works at the playhouses in London."

"Yes, but he travels England with a troupe this summer," Will said.

Edmund smiled. "I'm happy to meet you, especially on this joyous occasion. Please pardon my haste, but my affairs are so tangled, I need to see Will now."

"It's time I went downstairs to find out what I must do before we leave for church," John said, and left.

Will gestured for Edmund to sit down. "And what is it that moves you with such speed?"

Edmund remained standing. "Just before I left the tour for Stratford, I got a message from London. Kate is quite ill and has taken to her bed. This would be bad enough, but she is also heavy with child. I'm already in deep with the money-lenders, but have no cash and must get to London to be at her side."

Will stood up. "God's body, man. Are you always in some bind?"

"I'm sorry, but . . ."

"You know I'll help with the money." He opened a desk drawer. "Do it the right way. Marry her, and get out of London. It's no place to raise children."

"I'm going to stay in London and be a player, just like you did."

"You're not just like me, and I'm not sure you want to be. You have to decide what's important to you and follow that ideal." Will emptied his purse into Edmund's hand. "I'll be back in London next week. Hopefully, all will be well with your Kate by then, and we'll talk about what to do next."

There was another knock and Gilbert walked in. "John said you two were up here. I didn't think you'd miss this day." He hugged Edmund. "Susanna would scold you the rest of your life. But you look as if you just rode in."

"I know. I've got to stop home and change clothes. Just lay off me, I have enough troubles. I'll meet up with you when we walk to church." Edmund left.

"I see Master Quickly still lives up to his reputation. What is it this time?" Gilbert asked.

"He has troubles awaiting him in London, great-bellied woman troubles." For a brief moment, Will thought of his wedding to Anne, when she was pregnant with Susanna. *Maybe Edmund really loves Kate.*

Gilbert raised an eyebrow. "You know Mother worries about him constantly. You could help by reassuring her that all is well. That is, if all is well."

"Edmund does what he wants. Much as we hate to admit it, he is his own man and makes his own choices." Will walked toward the door. "Mother will just have to put up with it. Let's go, the guests are beginning to arrive."

Gilbert and Will walked downstairs, right into the middle of a crowd which included Michael Drayton, whom Will had known in both Warwickshire and London. "I just saw *Macbeth*. A powerful story, but I see you didn't spare our King. How did he like it?" Michael asked .

"I think the witches were his favorite part. Does Prince Henry like the poems you wrote for him?"

"Much better than his father, who took no notice of the one I composed for his coronation."

"This is too nice a day to ruin it with talk of the King," Will said.

"Even the Queen would agree with you," Michael said with laughter.

With the arrival of Will and Gilbert, the crowd moved to the living room, where a hushed quiet fell over the guests who stood and waited for the fun to begin. The young men started an exchange of short verses filled with rhyme and ridicule, after which John Hall gave them small gifts. Then the clamor of happy guests filled the room again. A dozen servants circulated among them with trays of delectable goodies.

"I have sweet meats and cakes for you, Master Shakespeare," Liddy said.

"My thanks, I'm hungry. I see Hamnet and Judith Sadler in the garden. Have they been here long?"

"They brought the cakes earlier and just came back with some of their children. Their married children are here too," Liddy said. "They asked for you. Go see them and I'll bring you some ale."

Susanna had remained in her room dressing while her bridesmaids went back and forth all morning, fixing their clothes and hair, helping her, then strolling around the house and gardens to be seen by the others. The sun was already warming the day when the bells from Holy Trinity Church rang out the call to unite the couple. Guests began the procession from New Place, singing the joy of the moment along with players of lutes, flutes and viols. John's young cousin who held a large silver cup of spiced wine accompanied Susanna. She looked like an angel with her shiny blonde hair worn straight to her waist and crowned with a garland of flowers. The lace and embroidered silk dress cinched her tiny waist and flared stylishly at the hip. Young boy cousins held white ribbons that were tied on her sleeves. Behind this gathering, the colorfully dressed bridesmaids surrounded John and accosted him with warnings of lost freedom. The bridesmaids carried small bridal cakes which would be shared after the ceremony.

The family took their places in the first row of the church while Susanna and John stood facing each other in front of the minister.

Susanna blushed as she said her vows. John placed the wedding ring firmly on her slim finger and didn't blush when he stated his intentions to be her dutiful husband. With that, the groomsmen rushed forward and pulled at the white ribbons on Susanna's sleeves. When each had taken his prize, the bridesmaids shared the cakes while Susanna and John drank from the processional cup. As the cup made the rounds, bells tolled and all cheered. The return procession was a merry parade, with the ringing of the bells emphasizing the family's happiness.

Six months later, the noon bells rang from another church and the mild summer Stratford weather gave way to a bitter London winter. Will was cold and found it hard to write even with the fire freshened. His new play was not coming along the way he wanted and he was disgusted. He'd changed the main story line three times and he still wasn't sure about it. Maybe revenge wasn't that important. But he knew it was.

He decided to seek out Edmund and have him help get more firewood. Edmund hadn't done well since Susanna's wedding. Kate and the baby both died in childbirth, and he'd been downcast for weeks at a time. Will often found him looking tired but he wasn't working. Perhaps a talk would help both of them.

Will rapped on the door of Edmund's room. There was no answer and he heard nothing inside. He rapped again, harder, and called Edmund's name. Finally, the landlady who lived in front came around.

"That deadbeat won't answer. I've been over here to get the rent and he don't ever answer at any time." She looked him over. "You a bill collector?"

"When did you last see him?" Will said.

"I don't keep track of my tenants, you know. A while. Maybe a week."

"Do you have a key? Maybe he left me a note. I'm his brother."

"You could be payin' his rent, then?"

"Yes, yes. The key?"

"Very well." She disappeared for a minute, then brought the key, and opened the door. A pungent smell assailed Will's nostrils. The room was cold and dirty.

"Edmund, Edmund." Will saw an inert form on the bed.

"God have mercy," the landlady said. "I never had no one to die before."

Will leaned over the body and tried to turn his head. It was Edmund. He felt the cold neck. Nothing.

"It's no plague. No plague ever in my house," the landlady said.

Will backed away and looked around the room. If only his warnings had been stronger. If only Edmund had listened. If only . . . He shivered. "I'll be back to take care of the body and his things later today."

"What about the rent?"

"I'll pay you his rent then."

"I'll be here. Make it soon. Got to clean up and rent this place to someone with better luck. Don't you go tellin' anyone it was plague, now."

Will sighed. "No, it's not plague. My brother died of a broken heart and lost dreams."

Chapter 21

London

1608

"Thus the whirligig of time brings in his revenges."
Taming of the Shrew

On Sunday morning, Will was free to do anything he wanted. He felt the need to walk. The crisp air and bright sun felt good and he looked into the faces of those he passed to read their mood. It was late enough that many were on their way home from church. After a half hour of walking in his neighborhood, it struck him that he hadn't met anyone he knew. Briefly, he considered stopping at Richard's or Cuthbert's, or even Richard Field's, but lately they were all busy with growing families. He couldn't think of anyone he could easily see and, because it was Sunday, The George was closed. He walked down to the river and he could see the roof of the Globe. It had become as important in his life as some of his relationships, yet disturbing things were happening there.

Thievery had become a problem since so much money flowed into their coffers. Will would sneak behind the box office at odd times to discover who was stealing. Other times, he counted their receipts every hour. Finally, he convinced Cuthbert that some company member had to stand guard at all times. Besides the money thefts, the groundlings had become violent. Fights were more common than ever, and a young apprentice was killed just a fortnight ago.

The Burbages' other playhouse, Blackfriars, had captivated another segment of the London audience and Will tried to write a different style of play for them. He struggled with the stories and the words. To add to that, the royal family wanted to be entertained by The King's Men frequently, and the performances were often very unusual. The royals always seemed distracted during plays unless the scene involved drinking or dancing. He wanted to talk to Richard about this.

The following week, they met at The George. Richard's first inquiry was about new plays.

"I have one I call *The Tempest*," Will said.

"Will it be ready for the royal performances?" Richard gulped his ale and chewed his food at the same time.

"Of course. Why the concern?"

"You haven't written anything for a while. Or is it just taking you a long time? God, I hope it's not as long as *Hamlet*."

Will slammed down his flagon. "You never quit harping, do you?"

"We need new plays, and Cuthbert is concerned."

"The *Tempest* is so good, we'll be able play it often. It's from pamphlets about the New World, Ovid's *Metamorphoses*, and John Florio's translation of Montaigne."

"Sounds like quite a concoction you're brewing."

"The witches in Macbeth couldn't have done better. Boil, boil, toil and trouble. Ask me for more, I'll turn you to rubble."

Richard stopped chewing. "It must be a great play to put you into such a good mood."

"The King probably won't sit still long enough to know if he likes it."

It only took a few rehearsals to be ready for a royal performance. As soon as the King and Queen sat down, the players blew out the candles surrounding the stage and blasted the room with smoke, claps of thunder from drums, wind whistling, crashing waves and the splintering wood and shouts one imagines in a shipwreck. Men ran back and forth in the panic of a ship sinking. Both the King and Queen paid attention, at least for a while. The characters Caliban and Trinculo drew laughter, Ferdinand and Miranda made the ladies sigh, and Ariel enchanted the Queen out of her usual stupor. When the masque started, she jumped from her seat and joined the players until Richard, as Prospero, escorted her back to her throne. She stayed there until the end when he gave up his magical powers, forgave his brother, and returned to family life in his homeland.

"Well played." The King and Queen both applauded.

Queen Anne put her hands together as if in prayer. "Oh, yes. The masque, it was the best. It was late in the play, mind you, but lovely, lovely. And just right for a wedding. We may want to have them perform it again."

The King looked at his Queen. "What a splendid idea, my dear. Where is Master Shakespeare?" He scanned the area where the players had been and belched.

"Ah'm off to get 'im, Your Highness," said one of the young men who stood next to the throne.

Will came out from behind the screens and approached the royal couple with a proper bow.

"Ah'm especially touched by Prospero's words about forgiveness," the King said. "'Though with their high wrongs Ah am struck to the quick...' How does that go?"

Will completed the line for him:

'Yet with my nobler reason 'gainst my fury
Do I take part: the rarer action is
In virtue than in vengeance:'

"Ay, there it is. Such words. Such poetry. Ah must have one of my counsellors commit these lines to memory so Ah can use them on the more dastardly noblemen, whose purpose is sah often lost in vengeance."

Will smelled the sweet Greek wine on King James' breath. "Thank you, Your Majesty. I'm flattered that you're entertained by my words. They're my humble offering."

"Pray tell me, why did that fool Prospero break his staff and fling his book into the deep?" King James laughed. "Ah hope you weren't suggesting that Ah should do that with my sceptre of office and the Great Seal." The King gave him a devious look and scratched his crotch vigorously.

"Not at all, your Majesty. If there's any significance beyond entertainment, it's about me...

"... I'll break my staff,
Bury it certain fathoms in the earth,
And deeper than did ever plummet sound
I'll drown my book."

"'Drown the book,' you say? Do you mean t' quit writing?" The King asked.

"Your Majesty, my family lives in Stratford and would like to see me more often."

"Brin 'em tae London. The mair the merrier."

"Maybe his wife will tell him," the Queen said. "There's never enough dancing in his plays. He needs more masques."

"My Queen has spoken. We expect to have many mair plays from you, and a lot of masques." The King dismissed Will with a flick of his wrist.

Behind the screen, when the players were all packed up, Richard grabbed Will's arm:

"'Our revels now are ended.
These our actors,
As I foretold you, were all spirits and
Are melted into air, into thin air:
And, like the baseless fabric of this vision,
The cloud-capp'd towers, the gorgeous palaces,
The solemn temples, the great globe itself,
Yea, all which it inherit, shall dissolve
And, like this insubstantial pageant faded,
Leave not a rack behind. We are such stuff

As dreams are made on, and our little life
Is rounded with a sleep...'

...And will I dissolve with the Globe?" Richard asked.

"Hardly. Large round things take a long time to melt. Besides, characters of my invention and my own mortality are no more permanent than dreams."

"Such talk is morbid," Richard said.

Will laughed. "I'm not thinking of dying. I'm thinking like Prospero:

'...Sir, I am vexed;
Bear with my weakness; my old brain is troubled:
Be not disturbed with my infirmity:
If you be pleased, retire into my cell
And there repose: a turn or two I'll walk,
To still my beating mind.' "

"Why is your brain troubled?"

"My family grows impatient for me to spend more time in Stratford."

"London is too boring when you're not here."

"And they're unhappy with my absence. I can't win. Let's go to The George and report to our other master." They walked to the river bank, where they boarded a water taxi to Southwark. The ferrymen shouted, "Eastward ho!" and they were off into the clear, cool November night.

They saw Cuthbert as soon as they walked into The George.

Will was eager to tell him about their performance. "King James loved *The Tempest* so much he waited until his audience with me to fart." Will waved to Moll. "Even Queen Anne awoke from her slumber as soon as she saw the fairy dances. They reminded her of Ben Jonson masques."

"What did the King say?" Cuthbert asked.

"He wondered about the way everyone was forgiven at the end. I didn't reveal I was the one who needed forgiveness from Anne."

"What's that about?" Richard asked.

"One of my friends back home read her one of my sonnets and she suspected they weren't written for her."

"Have Puck fly in and tell Anne it was poetic invention," said Richard.

Cuthbert said, "Now let me tell you something about the play business that will make you happy. Our clerk summarized and compared our two venues. The Globe fills an average of four days out of six, and Blackfriars is almost that good. However, because of the higher admission at Blackfriars, it brings in twice as much money."

"And it's one third the size," Richard said.

"Exactly," Cuthbert said. "We need to concentrate on Blackfriars. So tell me, do you think *The Tempest* will fill Blackfriars?"

"Better than *Pericles, Cymbeline,* or *The Winter's Tale,*" Will said. "But Cuthbert, the difference between audiences at the Globe and Blackfriars troubles me." Will looked into his half-filled goblet.

"Fewer thieves at Blackfriars," Richard said.

"Different kind of thievery. It used to be that all kinds went to The Globe and rubbed shoulders. Now, the upper class goes to Blackfriars and the meaner sort fills the Globe. What are people coming to? This tires me and makes me want to return to my family."

Cuthbert said, "Will, all I hear is your guilty conscience talking. You've lived in London for the past twenty years."

"I go back to Stratford for visits, but not often enough."

"Sure, then you high-tail it back to London after a couple of days. We're making plenty of money here. Rather than send money to your family, why not bring your family to where the money is?"

"They're small-town folk. London scares them."

"Money buys a lot of security and peace of mind. You promised my father and our troupe your help, and three plays a year. You know you need Richard's help to write, and he's not leaving."

Richard rolled his eyes.

"Yes, but…"

"No buts. You love London and London loves you. You promised, so now you've got to deliver."

"Just as your brother Richard keeps our troupe afloat, my brother Gilbert keeps my Stratford family safe and sound. I suppose I can stay a while more."

Chapter 22

Stratford

1612

"Nature teaches beasts to know their friends."
Coriolanus

One bitter cold evening, Gilbert Shakespeare died in his sleep. After another rush trip from London, Will arrived in late evening in Stratford. In the morning, he helped Anne wrap the coarse black mourning fabric around the bannister. Servants hung more cloth from the windows and over chairs. Judith sat in silence on the foyer floor with both arms wrapped around her knees. She stared at the scene in front of her.

When they reached the end of the railing, Anne tucked in the last piece of cloth. "I never thought about Gilbert leaving to meet our maker. I didn't even have his burial shirt embroidered."

"Is that what you did so early this morning?" Will asked.

"I edged it with a gloving stitch. His favorite."

"That's all?" Will ran his hand across the coarse black fabric.

"Then I added the Shakespeare coat-of-arms."

"Oh, yes. He is entitled to that."

"Your father was proud that you obtained that honor for him."

"Actually, Father first applied many years ago, when business was booming, but then he let it lapse. I just renewed the application, and the rest is history."

"Of course, the coat of arms honors you too."

"Is that the kind of shirt I'm going to be buried in?"

"I suppose. Is that what you want?" Anne finished winding the black thread onto the spool.

"I want mine to be the same as Gilbert's."

Judith sniffled. "Father, Uncle Gilbert looked like you. With more hair."

"Gilbert was my twin. Now, perhaps I begin to know how you must have felt at Hamnet's funeral."

Judith stood up. "I'm going to get ready. I want to look nice to send Uncle Gilbert to be with Hamnet and Grandfather."

Will watched Judith climb the stairs. "I never thought of Hamnet being with Father," he said to her back. She kept going.

"Every death is a reminder," Anne said.

"I always thought of Hamnet as being in our house with us." Will pulled Anne to him. She wept on his shoulder.

Liddy came out of the kitchen. "Master Sadler is here with the funeral cakes. Do you want to see him?"

"Yes, of course." Gilbert's death seemed harder on Anne than Father's or Mother's. She was more quiet than usual. Will felt like he was prying every word from her.

He greeted his friend with a hug. "This is such an unexpectedly sad day. I hope we'll see you again this afternoon."

"Judith wanted to know if there was anything she could do for Anne?"

"She's managing, I think."

"He was like a brother to me, too," Hamnet said. He looked down at his feet, feeling awkward. "Especially after you left. He kind of filled your shoes."

"I know. He did everything for this family."

That afternoon, at the same time the play houses in London were sounding their trumpets, Holy Trinity Church was tolling its bell. After the bells, the clergyman, Vicar Edward Woolmer, led a short service next to the coffin in the front room of New Place before it was taken to the church. When he finished, everyone placed an evergreen sprig on the lid and sipped from the communal pot of wine. The few children in attendance received coins, and their elders were given gloves. Finally, the servants distributed rosemary to place on the coffin or in mourners' hat bands.

The pallbearers lifted the heavy wooden coffin and carried it to a horse-drawn wagon. As had become the Shakespeare custom, the young cousins stood in the wagon and held a black linen canopy above the casket. The street was full of black clad friends and neighbors, who joined the long, slow procession toward Holy Trinity Church.

Will took Anne's hand while they walked. "I never thought about Stratford without Gilbert."

"He joins your Father and Mother in Heaven, with Hamnet."

"I wish I could believe that."

At the church yard, a freshly-dug grave marked Gilbert's final resting place. Again, Vicar Woolmer read burial prayers and the mourners cast their rosemary sprigs onto the lowered casket.

Will was last. "Gilbert, you were to be my Horatio, but it seems I am yours. Good bye dear brother." Will returned to his place by Anne and took her hand again.

Elizabeth wriggled free of Susanna's grasp. The three-year-old ran to her grandfather. "Up, up, Grandpapa. Up."

"Elizabeth!" Susanna said.

Will reached down to pick her up. "It's all right, Susanna. When your Uncle Gilbert was about Elizabeth's age, we went to a funeral for one of our Lambert cousins, and Gilbert ran straight to Uncle Henry just like your little Queenie."

Will enjoyed her warmth.

"Where is Uncle Gilbert, Grandpapa?" she asked.

"He has gone away."

"Gone where?"

"To the undiscovered country, from whose bourn no traveler returns."

"Is that near London?" Elizabeth asked.

"A little farther, precious one. Your mother will explain it to you." Will set Elizabeth down and pointed her toward Susanna and John.

The service was over, so Will took Anne's arm and started back toward New Place. "Gilbert doubled for me in real life. Our family would have been hollow without him."

A small tear trickled down Anne's cheek. Oh, Will, she thought. You'll never know how much Gilbert meant to me.

Sometimes, Will sat at his desk for hours, writing letters and balancing his ledgers. London was never like this. He had time to think, to concentrate. He began to resent the work, but he was stuck doing it unless he found someone to replace Gilbert. He'd been able to hire a rent collector and sought counsel from his friend Thomas Combe, but there was no one in town to keep his books. This house, the tenants on his lands, and his investments kept him busy, but left him unsatisfied. In London, writing for the stage was his relief from mundane chores.

On nice days, Will worked a little in the garden. On cold, rainy days, he read about gardening and imagined himself outside. Early one morning, Will sat in his library reading *The English Husbandman*, a garden book he bought in London from Richard Field. The servant girl Liddy burst into the room with a terrified look on her face. "You had best come help Mistress Anne, sir. Master Richard doesn't wake up."

Once more, New Place was draped in black and Will helped Anne wrap the stair bannister. She was more talkative this time.

"Have you embroidered the collar for Richard's burial shirt already?" Will asked.

"His was done a long time ago." Anne held down the cloth with the flat of her palm and wrapped it around the bannister with her other hand.

"Does it bear the coat-of-arms?"

"Yes, of course. Why do you ask?"

"I just wondered because of the way he was different."

"He couldn't help that. In God's eyes we're all equal."

"Not on earth, we're not."

Anne looked at Will. "It's good we will be going to church after a remark like that."

The Shakespeares buried Richard near Gilbert in the churchyard at Holy Trinity. This time, however, only the family and a few friends gathered afterwards. Will's sister Joan Shakespeare Hart said, "I wonder how things would have turned out if Richard hadn't kicked that Bishop all those years ago."

"Maybe not much differently; it's hard to say. Here's a line from my play *Hamlet*:

... 'tis better to bear the ills we have than to fly to others we know not of."

"You wrote a play Hamlet, Hamnet, Hamlet? Which is it?"
"That question still gives me nightmares."

Chapter 23

Stratford

1612

"Look like the innocent flower, but be the serpent under 't."
Macbeth

Less than a week after Richard's funeral, a coach from London pulled up to New Place, and a lone traveler emerged holding a small bag. His knock was answered by Liddy. "Who shall I say presents himself?"

"I'm John Fletcher, come from London to see Master William Shakespeare about a play. He received a letter announcing my arrival, so he expects me." John was not a tall man, but slender and handsome. He was about the same age as the recently-departed Edmund Shakespeare.

"Master Shakespeare is in mourning. He buried his brother last week."

"I am most…"

Will moved into the doorway. "Hello, John. Please come in. I didn't expect you so soon."

"I pray your forgiveness for the untimeliness of my arrival, Master Shakespeare. I knew nothing…"

"Thank you for your concern. My brother Richard didn't speak all his life, so his final silence is not much of a change for us."

John picked up his small bag. "Perhaps I should stay at the inn tonight and return on the morrow."

"Not at all. Come in. We'll work as planned. But first, you need to wash off the grime from your journey. I'll have your bag brought to a room, along with some fresh water. Have the servant show you to my study when you're ready."

"Thank you kindly, Master Shakespeare." John Fletcher followed Liddy upstairs.

Will returned to the front room and sat with Anne by the fire. She continued her embroidery without looking up.

"Cuthbert wants another play. He sent a letter about it some time back, but I never answered, so he sent John Fletcher to press the issue. The work should go quickly. Actually, I already wrote a few things."

"London again. Your friends from there don't miss you, or they would visit. This is the first we see of any of them. It's only because they want your plays."

"Anne, the King and Queen grieve the death of their son, and they want me to write a play to make them feel better."

"It's a long time since I thought about Hamnet. No one wrote a play for us."

"I did."

"This is the first I've heard of it."

"It wasn't about him exactly, but it shared his name."

"So why didn't you tell me?"

"The play didn't turn out the way I first expected."

"I don't understand what you're saying," Anne said. "Maybe I need to see your plays if I'm ever going to figure you out."

"That would mean a lot to me."

She stood up and gave him a scornful look. "I'll get some food for your guest."

Will went upstairs to his study. He looked through the pile of correspondence in a drawer and located the letter from Cuthbert.

> *My Dearest Will,*
> *My dear friend, we miss you all the time, just as I said we would. This letter comes as a plea for your most able skills. Box office receipts are still fairly good, and we make frequent use of your plays, thanks be to our Lord.*

Most unhappily, we suffer with a saddened monarch who we feel obligated to entertain. Last month, Prince Henry became ill with a fever and did not respond to the best doctoring in the land. He died within four days, and his parents plunged into such melancholy humour that no one can distract their thoughts away from this. Prince Henry just became eighteen years old, and his training to be King had proceeded most admirably. King James' pleasure at him was something to behold, just as we all glory in our children when they perform as we wish. Yet, just as they might bring us joy, their early death brings great sorrow.

There are those who pray the pending marriage of their daughter, Lady Elizabeth, to the most worthy German Protestant Frederick, Elector Palatine, will cheer the King out of his sadness. We pray that the plays we present for that occasion will help. We do believe that after the wedding, we should continue to entertain our King and Queen with more plays designed to brighten them. We are in great need of one with much pomp and fancy dress. Richard says it should be about Henry so the name of the departed is prominent, but I leave that to you.

I will send John Fletcher soon after the holiday plays end. He is eager to work with you. At present, he and Francis Beaumont have written several goodly plays for us, and they are nice young men, but we need your words to cheer our King and change the mood of his people. I worry about our patron's well-being,. He always fancied you, so perhaps your words will console him.

As if that is not enough, since Robert Cecil died last spring, the King decided to address Parliament personally, and it turned into the worst disharmony for all concerned.

I make this request to you with some hesitation, but I pray you will indulge me this time. May the Lord be with you.

We look to the day when Richard and I might share a meal with you again.

With fondest regards,
Cuthbert Burbage xx
From Holywell the 15 December 1612.

Will put the letter down and looked at the large stack of foolscap on his desk. In his spare moments, he read Holinshed about Henry VIII and formed a good story. He even wrote a few tentative scenes. Maybe John Fletcher will have some worthy ideas and make the rest easy. Will closed his eyes and saw his Globe.

A firm knock on the study door woke him. "Come in."

John entered and looked around at all the books. "I know of no writer who has such a fine workshop."

"I wrote many plays in rough surroundings so that I could build this workshop." But then he thought to himself, where I never write.

"Cuthbert's letter outlined the general nature of this play for the King, so I sorted out some ideas for you to review," Will said.

"Cuthbert thinks the play should contain something about Henry, as the King would cherish that honor for his son."

"We have only one possibility, Henry VIII. I checked Holinshed. If you review what I wrote, we can alter the plot and whatever lines are necessary in the next few days. Then you could go back to London and get it into rehearsal soon. This will make the writing swift and the King and Cuthbert happy."

"That sounds ambitious, so I'd best get to work. Point out Holinshed's *Chronicles* in case I need it." John took some sheets of foolscap and sat down in one of the red leather chairs.

Will remembered the days when he was that intense. "Work as late as you like, and I'll see you tomorrow."

The following day, Will and Anne got up with the sun. When John Fletcher didn't appear at breakfast, Will went outside to his garden. Nothing was in bloom this time of year, but there was a lot of greenery. He cleared away some winter debris to give the plants freedom to grow. He turned at the sound of Anne's footsteps.

"It's not very warm yet," she said.

"It feels good as long as I keep moving."

"Too brisk for me. I won't stay long."

Will moved a loose pile of leaves and saw the young tips of crocuses, just showing. "Look at this, Anne. Our first spring flowers."

Anne knelt at his side. "I was just thinking about this play you're writing. I know you'll want to go to London to see it."

"A play is like a flower. If my play is that good, I'll be pleased," he said.

Anne laughed. "Only you would compare a flower and a play."

"That's how I see it. Why don't you come to London with me and maybe it will make more sense to you."

"London is too big and smelly for me."

"But I'll be there with you. You can see The Globe and meet my London friends."

"I don't think . . ."

"I'll hire the finest carriage, and we'll take Judith, Susanna and John, and make it a family event."

"Enough. It's cold out here."

"Go in and see if our guest is up yet. I'll follow shortly."

That afternoon, after dinner, Will and John went to Will's study to work on the play.

"I take great pleasure reading your poetry, but in this play, it appears the best parts are those of Cardinal Wolsey and Queen Katherine. King Henry looks like a dolt by comparison."

"Well, that stays close to the history," Will said.

"I suppose. But the separation of the Church of England from the Catholic Church is a small event in this play. Shouldn't we make it more important?"

"John, this play must be short and to the point because our monarchs pay little attention. Also, it must get past the Master of the Revels. I'm not sure how he would view the religious issue, and we don't want to risk delays."

"Yes, I see. That's why you only used Henry's early years when he was more sympathetic, but how can you end it with the christening of Elizabeth?"

"Listen," Will quoted:

'She shall be loved and fear'd; her own shall bless her;
and those about her
From her shall read the perfect ways of honour
And by those claim their greatness, not by blood.'"

He watched John's face for some reaction. "Do you feel it?"

"Ah, sweet reminders of our recently departed Queen," Fletcher nodded.

"Queen Elizabeth deserves this tribute," Will said.

"But this play is for her successor, who just underwent a profound sorrow." Fletcher sorted the foolscap until he found the sheet he wanted. "To bring King James into this play, I drafted an addition to Bishop Cranmer's speech." He stood up and read:

'So shall she leave her blessedness to one,
When heaven shall call her from this cloud of darkness,
Who from the sacred ashes of her honour
Shall star-like rise, as great in fame as she was'

Will shifted his weight and looked at John. "Do you think the audience will believe Archbishop Cranmer's gift of prophecy could extend all the way to James?"

"But he's our patron. We must include him."

Will looked down at the spots on his wrinkled hands. "You must live with our patron, while I'm far away, tending my garden. It's of much greater importance to you than me."

"Do you think we could do more to honor King James?" John Fletcher asked.

"I would sooner praise a toad."

"I beg your pardon?"

"Oh nothing, I wondered how this would play on the road."

John Fletcher packed up and left the following morning.

"So, this is the end of your plays?" said Anne.

"Your impatience is showing, my dear," said Will.

"Isn't it enough?"

"Anne, I don't want my last play to whitewash an immoral king with some youngster who knows little. I owe a better play to the British people whose loyalty has made our lives so comfortable. They need something inspirational, and I think I can give it to them."

"Why am I not surprised?"

"Please hear me out. My last play should be about the glorious days of England, not the current chaos."

"I suppose. What do you have in mind?"

"I've been reading an old Latin book by Geoffrey of Monmouth. Have you heard of Excalibur, Merlin, Mordred, and Guinivere?

"Of course, you're talking about King Arthur."

"You see? This play will be familiar to everyone."

"So, is it back to London for you, then?"

"No, I'll write it here. *Arthur, King of All Britons.*"

The absence of Richard Burbage to speak the lines, the helpful suggestions of John Florio, and the constant interruptions of estate matters handicapped Will, but he knew a strong first draft would carry the project far. Will worked hard and was gratified at the way the tricks of his craft hadn't deserted him. *Arthur* was no two-week wonder like *The Merry Wives of Windsor*, but it didn't take long to assemble a version that was suitable for the copy-makers to work on so it could move on to the next phase.

Chapter 24

Stratford, then London

1613

"The play's the thing wherein I'll catch the conscience of the king."
Hamlet

Arthur, King of All Britons was finished by May. Will knew it would need some revisions after Richard had his say, but he thought they would be minor.

"Anne, it's done. My best play ever. I am so pleased."

"I suppose you'll go to London to deliver it."

"Well, there is only this one copy, so . . ."

"I have a suggestion. We're not getting any younger, so maybe this is the time to take up your offer to make a trip to London as a family."

Will was incredulous. "Do you really mean that?"

"Yes I do. Susanna and John, Judith, and you and me should all travel to London and see the play you and that fellow John Fletcher, who came to Stratford, wrote last year. The plays have provided a fine life for us. We need to see what they are all about."

"*Henry VIII* will be played next month, but I'm flabbergasted that you're willing to go to the city you dislike with so much venom."

"It's the place that pulled you away from us for so long. This way, we could get a real idea about how you spent your time there and meet some of your friends. Possibly it will make me less bitter about your absence."

"Perhaps that would happen and I could be forgiven. And you'd see how my words sound when professionals speak them. It would be lovely."

Will could barely believe his ears. Anne willing to go to London? Maybe she might begin to understand his passion for the stage. Richard Burbage and John Florio would certainly help win her over. Cuthbert? Well, maybe. At least she wouldn't have to put up with the King and Queen. Perhaps she wouldn't mind if he made a few trips to London to make sure *Arthur* got a good start on stage.

In late June, Will and his two daughters stood in front of New Place. Will held the door to the hired coach for Susanna and Judith. "What's taking your mother so long?"

"She keeps going back for things," Susanna said. "I think maybe she's afraid to leave."

"I'm afraid of what London holds for us, but I'm all ready to go," Judith said.

"John went in to calm her," Susanna said.

This was a new experience for the women who had never gone beyond nearby Warwick. Will and John had warned them about the stomach-wrenching jolts and mouth-drying dust that made a long coach ride difficult. Hours later, when they stopped at Grendon Underwood to spend their first night, they welcomed the chance to wash off the grime and rest their bones. Will's friends at the Ship Inn were thrilled to meet his kinfolk and included them at their family table.

The next evening in London, Anne liked their accommodations at the Golden Lion and began to relax. That night, everyone slept soundly on thick straw beds covered in soft linen. At breakfast, they planned the day. They started out by walking through the London shops where shopkeepers tempted them with the finest goods imported from the Far East and the continent. Judith found gifts for everyone back in Stratford while Anne and Susanna bought fine china and clocks for their houses.

They had to be coaxed into stopping early for a meal so they wouldn't be late to the playhouse. They ate at the Inn, and Will promised them a real playgoers dinner at The George the next day.

Finally, they arrived at the Globe.

"It's so big," Anne said. "I had no idea it would be this large."

"I love the colorful banners, Daddy," Susanna said.

As they entered, many people greeted Will warmly. Once inside, Will settled the family in a lord's box on cushioned seats where they could watch the stage and the audience. "I'm going to see my friend Richard Burbage. I'll return before the play starts."

In the tiring house, Will greeted Richard with a bear hug and a slap on the back.

Richard laughed and said, "You're beginning to look as well-fed as Falstaff."

"I don't have the London streets to walk, and Anne makes me regular banquets. You seem a little slimmer."

"Cuthbert works me pretty hard, and Winifred always has much for me to do at home."

Will gave Richard a tied bundle of foolscap. "Take my new play and read it through. It's my best work and you'll love your part."

"Is it *Arthur King of All Britons*? Finished?"

"Almost. Read through it for me, and make your marks. I'll take it back to Stratford and finish it."

"I hope you're going to be here for a while. We've got a new play starting at Blackfriars, and we're rehearsing every spare minute. I have the next week totally filled."

"What about Sunday?"

"Oh, you must not have gotten my letter. John Florio knew you were coming, and his Italian tutoring of the Queen will get a palace invitation so your family can meet the King and Queen on Sunday, after church."

Will gasped. "I... I..." Not what he was hoping for.

"Before I hurry on stage, I've got to tell you something disturbing. *Henry VIII* isn't like most of your plays."

"What is different?"

"You know how Hamlet told his players that the words should sound 'Trippingly off the tongue?' Well, many of these lines don't flow very trippingly."

"Really?"

"And, there's a cannon fired in Act I."

"A cannon? Are the groundlings at war?"

"They fire it on the second floor in the tiring house, and use paper wadding so no one gets hurt. Still, cannon fire in this wooden Globe scares me."

"That wasn't in the play I sent here with John Fletcher."

"Anyway, you should talk to Cuthbert. I've got to get going."

Will found Cuthbert in the box office. He looked older. He was slightly stooped and the lines in his face were more deeply etched. "Richard says the play I sent was changed considerably."

"Oh, yes. John Fletcher fixed it very well."

"Fixed it? What was wrong?"

"Some of the lines were too poetic, there wasn't enough praise for King James, and it was way too long."

"What about the cannon?"

"We needed that to capture the groundlings' attention."

Will just shook his head. Was he unhinged? "Well, Cuthbert, I just delivered the only draft of my best play to date, *Arthur, King of all Britons*. I need Richard to look it over to help with the lines."

"Fine news. I'm sure John Fletcher will be able to patch it up, and we'll make plenty of money with it."

Will stared at him, wide-eyed. "That it should come to this!" He started to deliver a few choice words when a single trumpet blast signaled that the play was almost ready to start. Will turned and trudged his way toward the lord's box where Anne, Susanna, John, and Judith awaited.

Susanna grabbed both of Judith's hands. "You must sit in front where everyone can see you. Maybe a young man will notice you and ask Father if he could spend time with us."

"Susanna!" Anne said. "How can you say such things? We're here to see Father's play."

"Father says people come here to be seen as well as see the plays."

"Now that I finally got your father to spend more time at home, I certainly don't want my daughter courting in London."

"Look!" John pointed. "There are players out there."

They watched two men stretch and dance across the stage, oblivious to the early arrivals. One stopped mid-stage and yelled senseless lines to the almost empty pit and gallery. They disappeared when five trumpeters stood on the balcony above and blasted the opening announcement. Will came in and sat down.

They watched loud and happy patrons carrying food and drink crowd their way into the pit in front of the stage. The seats were slower to fill.

"I've never seen so many people in one place," Judith said. "Do you know how many there are?"

"Fifteen hundred," Will said.

Then the trumpeters appeared a second time to sound the opening of the play and a lone narrator appeared at stage center:

I come no more to make you laugh; things now
That bear a weighty and serious brow, . . .

Will whispered to Anne. "I've never sat up here."

"Where did you watch from?"

"I stayed in the tiring house and paced. I never sat anywhere."

"But the audiences liked your plays."

"Most of them. Not always."

There was silence everywhere for the prologue, but when the Dukes of Buckingham and Norfolk, and Lord Abergavenny came on stage to talk about their distrust of Cardinal Wolsey, the groundlings started.

"Bugger the French."

"Don't trust no churchman."

"Do they always yell?" Anne asked.

"If they're interested."

The story moved quickly. "You see the King, Anne? That's Richard Burbage."

"He's shorter than I thought."

"He's such a good actor, he makes you think he's tall."

"Daddy," Susanna said, "Why is he so mean to Katherine?"

"Shh. I can't listen when you talk," Anne said.

"Everyone else is talking," Susanna said.

"That's why I can't hear."

"We'll talk about it later," Will said

"Who's the girl?" John asked.

"Anne Boleyn."

"Really?" Anne asked. "Did you name her for me?"

"No need. History did it." He chuckled. "Watch how she gets along with the King."

"She's really a boy?" John said.

"She sounds like a girl," Judith said.

"You and Hamnet sounded alike when you were young," Will said. "They do until their voices change."

"Shh," Anne said.

Just then, a cannon went off with a loud booming noise that shook the playhouse.

"I hate that noise," Will said. He held his ears.

"Look, it's Master Burbage, wearing a mask," Anne said. "Do kings wear disguises?"

"Yes, now watch what he does," Will said.

King Henry walked toward the lovely Anne Boleyn:

"The fairest hand I ever touch'd! O beauty,
Till now I never knew thee!"

"Daddy, what about . . ." Judith said.

"Hush, child. This is an important part."

The King kissed Anne Boleyn on the lips, then all danced off the stage as if the evening was young and there was much ahead.

"Your friend Richard really kissed that young boy?" John said.

"It's make-believe and that's the joy of plays," Will said. "Now, what did you want, Judith?"

"There is smoke up on the roof."

Will looked up at the thatched roof that stood high against the beautiful summer sky. Wisps of smoke curled around its edges, fanned by a breeze. He looked back down and saw the groundlings also looking up. The stage was strangely empty.

"God's mercy, child, it is smoke!" Will stood up. "Let's get out of here."

"Is there fire?" Anne asked.

John stood up. "Maybe that cannon . . ."

"Out. Now." Will grabbed Judith's hand. "Run down the stairs and get out of the building. Hurry."

Suddenly, everyone was moving. Actors poured out of the tiring house, onto the stage, and into the aisles, dancing a sort of quick-time Morris step. Richard came out to stage center and raised his scepter. There was a fanfare of trumpets from behind.

"Ladies and gentlemen, we shall continue this dance in the next chamber, outside with you all," Richard said. "Be quick about it, your King commands you. GO NOW!"

When the children were safely out, Will turned back to get Anne. He pulled her by the arm and ran down the first few steps. She tripped and fell towards him. Will caught her and steadied himself, but she laid limp in his arms. Will made his way down practically dragging her. Once on solid footing, he picked her up. The smoke was thick and he could feel it entering his lungs. Thank heavens he knew his way. She didn't weigh very much, but her skirts made her large and awkward. He heard the desperate yelling of others, trying to find loved ones. Will maneuvered his way outside.

Then he yelled. "John, Susanna, Judith. Over here." There was no answer, only the shouts and the crackling and crashing of the old timbers he had so painfully slid across the frozen Thames.

Will carried Anne across the street where he found a patch of grass away from the fleeing crowd. He put his ear to her mouth and felt her faint breath. He loosened the button at her neck and whispered. "Anne, don't go now. Stay with me." Nothing. He looked her over. She appeared younger than her years. Then he saw the blood on his sleeve. He felt his arm, but nothing hurt. He looked Anne over more carefully. He touched a wet spot on her hair and felt the solidity of her skull. She must have hit her head on the railing.

He stood up and looked around, then yelled at the top of his lungs. "John Hall. John Hall. Do you hear me?"

Nothing. He kneeled again and made sure she was still breathing. He took off his doublet and put it under her head. "I have to get help."

Will ran back to the street where the smoke was so thick he couldn't see anyone. He shouted again. This time, John answered. He was huddled with Susanna and Judith. They met and ran back to Anne, who had opened her eyes.

John knelt at her side and ran his fingers over her head. He looked in her eyes and asked her a few questions. Anne coughed and spoke in a faint voice.

"She's all right," John said. "She hit her head, but it's not too bad. She must stay quiet for a few days."

Behind him, he heard a crash. He turned and saw black smoke and sparks billowing high above them. The entire Globe was aflame.

"Move quickly. To the river bank," Will said. "Together we'll carry her. I know the way."

Anne moaned when they picked her up.

"You'll be all right," John said. "We're moving you to a safe place."

Her eyes were open and she whispered something.

"Susanna and Judith are right here," John said. "Don't talk anymore."

They carried Anne the short distance to a flat clearing next to the Thames. People were everywhere, and the fire made a roaring noise in the background. The air was full of black specks and Will's lungs hurt. John and the girls went off to find a coach, leaving Will at Anne's side. He stroked her hand. "I'm sorry, Anne. Please forgive me."

She opened her eyes and smiled.

"Will, Will." Cuthbert Burbage stood above them. "I've looked all over for you. Thank the Lord you're all right."

"I think so," Will said.

"I must meet with you as soon as this cursed fire is out. Come by my house tonight."

"I can't," Will said. "I'll be with Anne."

"Who?" Cuthbert asked.

"My wife," Will didn't even look up.

"Oh yes, I heard your family was here." He looked at Anne. "Is she all right?"

"I don't know. I need to take her home so she can rest."

"We need to plan rebuilding and rewriting. All the play scrolls and your new *Arthur* play were burnt in the tiring house."

"Not now Cuthbert. You have no more authority over me."

"Can I get you at least to commit some money? We need £100 from you. Come help us rebuild, Will."

Will tilted his head back and looked at Cuthbert squarely. His eyes blazed. After a brief pause, he said, "Cuthbert you disgust me. Your emphasis on money sounds more like my father than yours. Life isn't about money, it's about love. The love of my life and I are going home."

Thank you for reading this book.

If you would be willing to help us, please consider writing a review for Amazon, Goodreads, or LibraryThing.

Any comments, questions, or criticisms can be directed to bart4bard@gmail.com

BONUS:

Shoot a selfie holding the book, e-mail it to us, and we'll post it on
www.shakespearenovel.com

To Dig Deeper

Perhaps this knowledge of Will's life merely whets your appetite for more. An amazing lode of detailed information has been written over the many years since Will lived, and there has been considerable speculation about events that haven't been recorded.

To assist your possible interest, here are several appendices that may help in your quest to learn more.

The Shakespeare Family Tree During Will's Lifetime

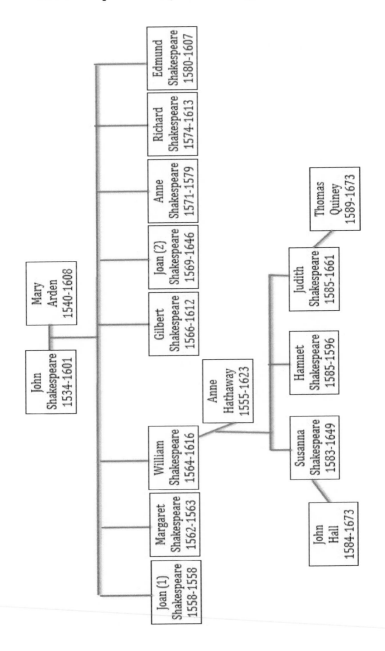

Familiar Lines from Shakespearean Plays

All the world's a stage, and all the men and women merely players. They have their exits and their entrances; And one man in his time plays many parts.
As You Like It, Act II, Scene 7

Frailty, thy name is woman
Hamlet I, 2

To thine own self be true
Hamlet I, 3

Something is rotten in the state of Denmark
Hamlet I, 4

There are more things in heaven and earth, Horatio, than are dreamt of in your philosophy
Hamlet I, 5

Nothing either good or bad, but thinking makes it so
Hamlet II, 2

What a piece of work is a man
Hamlet II, 2

Brevity is the soul of wit
Hamlet II, 2

Get thee to a nunn'ry
Hamlet III, 1

The lady doth protest too much, methinks
Hamlet III, 2

To be, or not to be, that is the question
Hamlet III, 1

Hold as 'twere the mirror up to nature
Hamlet III, 2

Speak the speech, I pray you, trippingly on the tongue
Hamlet III, 2

In my heart of heart
Hamlet III, 2

Sweets to the sweet
Hamlet V, 1

Alas, poor Yorick! I knew him, Horatio
Hamlet V, 1

The better part of valor is discretion
1 Henry IV V, 4

He hath eaten me out of house and home
2 Henry IV II, 1

Uneasy lies the head that wears the crown
2 Henry IV III, 1

Let's kill all the lawyers
2 Henry VI IV, 2

Yond Cassius has a lean and hungry look
Julius Caesar I, 2

Beware the Ides of March
Julius Caesar I, 2

But, for my own part, it was Greek to me
Julius Caesar I, 2

The fault, dear Brutus, lies not within the stars, but in ourselves, that
we are underlings
Julius Caesar I, 2

A dish fit for the gods
Julius Caesar II, 1
Cowards die many times before their deaths; the valiant never taste
of death but once.
Julius Caesar II, 2

Cry "havoc" and let slip the dogs of war
Julius Caesar III, 1

How sharper than a serpent's tooth it is to have a thankless child!
King Lear I, 4

Screw your courage to the sticking place
Macbeth I, 7

What's done, is done
Macbeth III, 2

Something wicked this way comes
Macbeth IV, 1

One fell swoop
Macbeth IV, 3

Out, damn'd spot
Macbeth V, 1

To-morrow, and to-morrow, and to-morrow, creeps in this petty
pace from day to day, to the last syllable of recorded time
Macbeth V, 5

Life's but a walking shadow, a poor player, that struts and frets his hour upon the stage, and then is heard no more; it is a tale told by an idiot, full of sound and fury, signifying nothing
Macbeth V, 5

All that glisters is not gold
The Merchant of Venice II, 7

A blinking idiot
Merchant of Venice II, 9
If you prick us, do we not bleed? If you tickle us, do we not laugh? If you poison us, do we not die? And if you wrong us, shall we not revenge?
Merchant of Venice III, 1

The quality of mercy is not strain'd
Merchant of Venice IV,1

The course of true love never did run smooth
A Midsummer's Night's Dream I, 1

Lord, what fools these mortals be
A Midsummer's Night's Dream III, 2

The green-ey'd monster which doth mock the meat it feeds on
Othello III, 3

Pride, pomp, and circumstance of glorious war
Othello III, 3

I am one who loved not wisely but too well.
Othello V, 2

Now is the winter of our discontent
Richard III I, 1

The King's name is a tower of strength
Richard III V, 3

A horse, a horse! My kingdom for a horse
Richard III V, 4

Romeo, Romeo! wherefore art thou Romeo?
Romeo and Juliet II, 2

What's in a name? A rose by any other name would smell as sweet
Romeo and Juliet II, 2

What light through yonder window breaks
Romeo and Juliet II, 2

A wild-goose chase
Romeo and Juliet, II 4

A plague a' both your houses
Romeo and Juliet III,1

What's past is prologue
The Tempest II, 1

We are such stuff as dreams are made on, and our little life is rounded with a sleep
The Tempest IV, 1

Brave new world
The Tempest V, 1

We have seen better days
Timon of Athens IV, 2

If music be the food of love, play on
Twelfth Night, I, 1

Some are born great, some achieve greatness, and some have
greatness thrust upon them
Twelfth Night II, 5

Play and Poem Chronology (Approximate) and Possible Sources

Edward III
1st Quarto Edition 1589-95
*Froissart, Jean (c.1337-1410). *Chroniques* (c.1495) (John Bourchier's English translation in 1523-5)
*Painter, William (1540-94). *The Palace of Pleasure* (1566-7)
*Holinshed, Raphael (c. 1528-c. 1580). *The Chronicles of England, Scotland and Ireland. (2nd ed., 1587)*

Two Gentlemen of Verona 1589-93
*Giovanni Boccaccio (1313-75). *Decameron* 10th day, the story of *Titus and Gisippus*
*Elyot, Thomas (c.1490-1546). *The Booke named the Governour* (1531)
*Montemayor, Jorge de (c.1521-61). Diana Enamorada (1542, English translation in 1582. publication in 1598) the story of *Felix and Felismena*
*Anonymous. *The History of Felix and Philiomena* (the record of the performance in 1585)
*Brooke, Arthur (?-1563). *The Tragical History of Romeus and Juliet* (English translation in 1562)
*Lyly, John (c.1554-1606). *Euphues* (1578)

The Taming of the Shrew 1593-94
*Anonymous ballad. *A Merry Jest of a Shrewede and Curste Wyfe* (printed 1550)
*Gascoigne, George (1542-77). *Supposes* (performed 1566, published 1573, 1587. Translation of Italian drama , *I suppositi* (1509)
*Anonymous. *The Taming of a Shrew* (1594) SR(2.May.1594)
*the influence of Commedia dell'arte

2 Henry VI 1591
*Hall, Edward (1498-1547). *The Union of the Two Noble and Illustre Families of Lancaster and York* (3rd. ed., 1550)
*Fabyan, Robert (?-1513). *New Chronicles of England and France* (1516)

*Holinshed, Raphael (c. 1528-c. 1580). *The Chronicles of England, Scotland and Ireland. (2nd ed., 1587)*

*Grafton, Richard (c.1512-c.1572). *A Chronicle at Large of History of the Affayres of England* (1516)

*Hardyng, John (1378-c.1465). *The Chrocicle of John Hardyng* (1543)

*Foxe, John (1516-87). *The Book of Martyrs* (4th ed., 1583)

3 Henry VI 1592

*Hall, Edward (1498-1547). *The Union of the Two Noble and Illustre Families of Lancaster and York* (3rd. ed., 1550)

Holinshed, Raphael (c. 1528-c. 1580). The Chronicles of England, Scotland and Ireland. (2nd ed., 1587)*

*William Baldwin ed. *The Mirror for Magistrates* (1559 ed.)

*Edmund Spenser (c.1552-99). *The Faerie Queene* (1590) - descriptions of the sun at 2.1.

*Brooke, Arthur (?-1563). *The Tragical History of Romeus and Juliet* (English translation in 1562) - Queen Margaret's speech at 5.4.

*Kyd, Thomas (1558-94) *The Spanish Tragedy* (1588-9) and Soliman and Perseda (1590)

Titus Andronicus 1593-94

*a chapbook of "Titus Andronicus" sold by chapmen.

*Ovid (43 BC- AD18). *Metamorphoses* (Arthur Golding's English translation in 1567)

*Seneca, Lucius *Annaeus (4. BC-AD65). Thyestes* (English translation in 1560)

1 Henry VI 1590-92

*Hall, Edward (1498-1547). *The Union of the Two Noble and Illustre Families of Lancaster and York* (3rd. ed., 1550)

*Holinshed, Raphael (c. 1528-c. 1580). *The Chronicles of England, Scotland and Ireland. (2nd ed., 1587)*

*Fabyan, Robert (?-1513). *New Chronicles of England and France* (1516)

Richard III 1593

*Holinshed, Raphael (c. 1528-c. 1580). *The Chronicles of England, Scotland and Ireland*. (2nd ed., 1587)
*Hall, Edward (1498-1547). *The Union of the Two Noble and Illustre Families of Lancaster and York* (1587 edition)
*More, Thomas. *History of King Richard the Thirde*. (1543)
*William Baldwin ed. *The Mirror for Magistrates* (1559 ed.)

Venus and Adonis 1593

*Ovid (43 BC- AD18). *Metamorphoses* (Arthur Golding's English translation in 1567) Book 10.

The Rape of Lucrece 1594

*Ovid (43 BC- AD18). *Fasti* Book 2. (Latian version)
*Titus Livius (59BC-AD17). *Ab urbe condita libri* Book 1. (Latin)
*Painter, William (1540-94). *The Palace of Pleasure* (1566-7)
*Geoffrey Chaucer (c.1340-1400). *The Legend of Good Women* (c. 1386)

The Comedy of Errors 1589-94

*Plautus (c.254-184 BC). *Menaechmi* (perfromed 1592 with English translation by William Warner, printed 1595)
*Plautus (c.254-184 BC). *Amphitryon* (Latin)
*George Gascoigne (1542-77). *Supposes* (performed 1566, published 1573, 1587. Translation of Italian drama , *I Suppositi* (1509)
*the influence of Commedia dell'arte

Love's Labour's Lost 1594

No written source for the plot has been found.
*the influence of Commedia dell'arte

A Midsummer Night's Dream 1595

No written source for the plot has been found and it seems that the plot is Shakespeare's original. However, there are influences from the following:
Theseus and Hippolyta

*Plutarch (c.46-120). *Lives* (Thomas North's translation in 1579)
*Chaucer, Geoffrey (c.1340-1400). *The Canterbury Tales* "The Knight's Tale" (1400)
The story of "Pyramus and Thisbe" and the name of Titania.
*Ovid (43 BC- AD18). *Metamorphoses* (Arthur Golding's English translation in 1567)
Oberon
Huon of Bordeau, a 13th-century French adventure tale translated by Lord Berners (1534)

The Sonnets 1593-1603
There are no singular source, however, Shakespeare might have been influenced by the following.
*Daniel, Samuel (c.1562-1619). *Delia* (1592) distructive "Time"
*Sidney, Philip (1554-86). *Astrophel and Stella* (1591)
*indirectly but the inference of Francesco Petrarca (1304-74)

Romeo and Juliet 1594
*Brooke, Arthur (?-1563). *The Tragical History of Romeus and Juliet* (English translation in 1562)

Richard II 1595
*Hall, Edward (1498-1547). *The Union of the Two Noble and Illustre Families of Lancaster and York* (3rd. ed., 1550)
*Holinshed, Raphael (c. 1528-1580). *The Chronicles of England, Scotland and Ireland.* (2nd ed., 1587)
*Anonymous. *Thomas of Woodstock* (c. 1592)
*Froissart, Jean(c.1337-1410). *Chroniques* (1495?)(John Bourchier's English translation in 1523-5)
*William Baldwin ed. *The Mirror for Magistrates* (1559 ed.)
*Daniel, Samuel (c.1562-1619). *The Civil Wars between the Two Houses of Lancaster and York* (1595-1609)

King John 1590-95
*Anonymous. *The Troublesome Raigne of John King of England2 Vol.* (1591)

*Holinshed, Raphael (c. 1528-c. 1580). *The Chronicles of England, Scotland and Ireland.* (2nd ed., 1587)
*Foxe, John (1516-87). *The Book of Martyrs* (4th ed., 1583)

The Merchant of Venice 1596
*Fiorentino, Ser Giovanni *Il Pecorone* (The Simpleton) (1558)
*<u>Gesta Romanorum (1340, translation by Richard Robinson, 1595 ed)</u>
*a Lost English play The Jew
*Marlowe, Christopher (1564-93). *The Jew of Malta* (c. 1589)
*Munday, Anthony, *Zelauto* (1580)

1 Henry IV 1596
*Holinshed, Raphael (c. 1528-c. 1580). *The Chronicles of England, Scotland and Ireland.* (2nd ed., 1587)
*Daniel, Samuel (c.1562-1619). *The Civil Wars between the Two Houses of Lancaster and York* (1595-1609)
*Anonymous. *The Famous Victories of Henry the Fifth* (c. 1586)
*William Baldwin ed. *The Mirror for Magistrates* (1559 ed.)
*Stow, John (1525-c.1605) *The Chronicles of England* (1580)

The Merry Wives of Windsor 1597
There are no particular source for the plot, however, Shakespeare might have gotten inspirations and been influenced by the following:
*Fiorentino, Ser Giovanni *Il Pecorone* (The Simpleton) (1558)
*Ovid (43 BC- AD18). *Metamorphoses* (Arthur Golding's English translation in 1567)
*Lyly, John (c.1554-1606). *Endimion* (1588)

2 Henry IV 1597
*Holinshed, Raphael (c. 1528-c. 1580). *The Chronicles of England, Scotland and Ireland.* (2nd ed., 1587)
*Anonymous. *The Famous Victories of Henry the Fifth* (c. 1586)
*Hall, Edward (1498-1547). *The Union of the Two Noble and Illustre Families of Lancaster and York* (3rd. ed., 1550)

*Daniel, Samuel (c.1562-1619). *The Civil Wars between the Two Houses of Lancaster and York* (1595-1609)
*William Baldwin ed. *The Mirror for Magistrates* (1559 ed.)

Much Ado About Nothing 1598
*Ludovico Ariosto (1474-1533). *Orlando Furioso* (1516)(The English translation by John Harington in 1591)
*Bandello, Matteo (1485-1561) *Novelle* (1554-73) 22th story.
*Edmund Spenser (c.1552-99). *The Faerie Queene* (1590)
*Francois de Belleforest (1530-83). *Histories Tragiques* (1568) Book 3
*Whetstone, George *The Roke of Regard* (1576) -Clauido's rejection of Hero at her own wedding
*Castiglione, Baldassare (1478-1529) *The Book of the Courtier* (1528)

Henry V 1599
*Holinshed, Raphael (c. 1528-c. 1580). *The Chronicles of England, Scotland and Ireland*. (2nd ed., 1587)
*Anonymous. *The Famous Victories of Henry the Fifth* (c. 1586)
*Robert Fabyan (?-1513). *New Chronicles of England and France* (1516)
*Samuel Daniel (c.1562-1619). *The Civil Wars between the Two Houses of Lancaster and York* (1595-1609)

The Passionate Pilgrim 1599

Julius Caesar 1599
*Plutarch (c.46-120). *Lives* (Thomas North's English translation in 1579)
*Appian [Appianos] (2nd century). *Civil Wars* (English translation in 1578)
*Anonymous. *The Tragedy of Caesar and Pompey, or Caesar's Revenge* (c. 1595)

As You Like It 1599

*Thomas Lodge (c.1557-1625). *Rosalynde* (1590)

Hamlet 1600
*Thomas Kyd (1558-94). *Ur-Hamlet* (c. 1589)
*Francois de Belleforest (1530-83). *Histories Tragiques Book 5* (1570) (A translation of Saxo Grammaticus Gesta Danorum (History of the Danes) Books three and four)

Twelfth Night 1601
*Barnabe Riche (c.1540-1617). *Farewell to Militarie Profession* (1581) the story of "Apolonius and Silla"
*Bandello, Matteo (1485-1561) *Novelle* (1554-73)

The Phoenix and the Turtle 1601
There are no particular source, however, Shakespeare might have been influenced by the following;
*Chester, Robert Love's *Martyr* where <u>The Phoenix and the Turtle</u> appears
*Ovid (43 BC- AD18). *Amores* Book 2 6th poem.
*Matthew Roydon's elegy in *The Phoenix Nest*
*Chaucer, Geoffrey (c.1340-1400). The *Pralement of Foules*

Troilus and Cressida 1600-03
*Homer (c. 900.BC). *Iliad* (English translation in 1598 by George Chapman)
*Chaucer, Geoffrey (c.1340-1400). *Troilus and Criseyde* (c. 1385)
*Caxton, William (c.1421-91). *Recuyell of the Historyes of Troye* (1475, 5th ed. 1596)
*Lydgate, John (c.1370-1449). *The Troy Book* (1412-20, 1555 ed)

A Lover's Complaint 1603-04
*Samuel Daniel (c.1562-1619). *The Complaint of Rosamond* (1592)
*Edmund Spenser (c.1552-99). *Complaints* (1591)

Measure for Measure 1603
*George Whetstone (c.1544-87). *Promos and Cassandra* (1578)

*Cinthio, Giovanni Battista Giraldi.1504-73). *Hecatommithi* (1565. No English translations have found, therefore, Shakespeare probably read it either in Italian or French.)

*Barnabe Riche (c.1540-1617). *The Adventures of Brusanus, prince of Hungaria* (1592)--Lucio's interactions with the disguised Duke.

Othello 1602-03

*Cinthio (Giovanni Battista Giraldi.1504-73). *Hecatommithi* (1565. No English translations have found, therefore, Shakespeare probably read it either in Italian or French.) Book 2, 7th story of *"Disdemona and the Moor"*

*Pliny, the Elder (23-79). *Naturalia Historia* (Philemon Holland's translation in 1601)

*Africanus, Leo. *A Geographical History of Africa* (English translation by John Pory, 1600)

All's Well That Ends Well 1601-02

*Painter, William (1540-94). *The Palace of Pleasure* (1566-7)

Timon of Athens 1604-06

*Plutarch (c.46-120). *Lives* (Thomas North's English translation in 1579)

*Lucian (c. 120-180). *Timon, the Misanthrope* (No English translation which Shakespeare could use is found.)

*John Lyly (c.1554-1606). *Campaspe* (c. 1584)

*Anonymous. *Timon.* (c. 1602)

King Lear 1605

*Anonymous. *The True Chronicle History of King Leir* (c. 1590)

*Holinshed, Raphael (c. 1528-c. 1580). *The Chronicles of England, Scotland and Ireland.* (2nd ed., 1587)

*Sidney, Philip (1554-86). *The Arcadia* (1590)

*Spenser, Edmund (c.1552-99). *The Faerie Queene* (1590)

Macbeth 1606

*Holinshed, Raphael (c. 1528-c. 1580). *The Chronicles of England, Scotland and Ireland.* (2nd ed., 1587)

*Buchanan, George (1506-82) (1582)

*Seneca, Lucius Annaeus (4BC. - AD 65). *Hercules Furens and Agamemnon* (English translation in 1565)

Antony and Cleopatra 1607-08

*Plutarch's (c.46-120) *Lives* (Thomas North's translation in 1579)

*Appian [Appianos] (2nd century). *Civil Wars* (English translation in 1578)

*Daniel, Samuel (c.1562-1619). *The Tragedy of Cleopatra* (c. 1594)

Pericles 1606-07

*Gower, John (c. 1330-1408) *Confessio Amantis.* (1554 ed) which was from the medieval collection of Latin tales, *Gesta* Romanorum (c. 1340)

*Twine, Lurence (active 1564-1576) *The Patterne of Painefull Adventures* (1594, 1607)

*Sidney, Philip (1554-86). *The Arcadia* (1590)

Coriolanus 1608

*Plutarch (c.46-120). *Lives* (Thomas North's English translation in 1579)

*Livius, Titus or Livy (59BC-AD17). *Ab Urbe Condita Libri* (Philemon Holland's English translation as *The Romane Historie* in 1600.)

*Camden, William (1551-1623). *Remaines of Greater Worke Concerning Britain* (1605)

*Averell, William *A Marvaillous Combat of Contrarieties*

The Winter's Tale 1609

*Robert Greene (c.1558-92). *Pandosto* (1588)

*Ovid (43 BC- AD18). *Metamorphoses* (Arthur Golding's English translation in 1567)

Cymbeline 1609

*Holinshed, Raphael (c. 1528-c. 1580). *The Chronicles of England, Scotland and Ireland.* (2nd ed., 1587)
*William Baldwin ed). *The Mirror for Magistrates* (1559 ed.)
*Anonymous. *Frederyke of Jennen* 3rd ed., (1560)
*Anonymous. *The Rare Triumphs of Love and Fortune* (performed 158, printed 1589)
*Boccaccio, Giovanni (1313-75). *Decameron* 2nd Day, 9th story

The Tempest 1610

There are no particular source for the plot, however, Shakespeare might have gotten inspirations and be influenced by an event. In June 1609, the Sea Adventure was wrecked at Bermuda. A survivor William Strachey described his experience in a letter and his letter was circulated in manuscript.

*Strachey, William (c.1567-c.1634) (dated 15.Jul.1610, printed 1625)
*Jourdain, Sylvester (?-1650). *A Discovery of the Bermudas* (1610)
*Jourdain, Sylvester (?-1650) *The True Declaration of the Estate of Colonie in Virginia* (1610)

Henry VIII 1613

*Holinshed, Raphael (c. 1528-c. 1580). *The Chronicles of England, Scotland and Ireland.* (2nd ed., 1587)
*Foxe, John (1516-87). *The Book of Martyrs* (4th ed., 1583)

Reference Books

Ackroyd, Peter. *Shakespeare The Biography.* Doubleday, 2005.

Asimov, Isaac. *Asimov'e Guide to Shakespeare.* Avenal Books, 1970.

Ashley, Mike. *Shakespearean Detectives.* Carroll & Graf Publishers, 1998.

Atwood, Margaret. *Hag-seed.* Hogarth, 2016.

Bartlett, John. *The Complete Concordance to Shakespeare.* Palgrave Macmillan, 1969.

Bentley, Gerald Eades. *Shakespeare: A Biographical Handbook.* Yale University Press, 1961.

Blackwood, Gary. *The Shakespeare Stealer.* Puffin Books, 1998.

Bloom, Harold. *Shakespeare: The Invention of the Human.* Riverhead Books, 1999.

Boyce, Charles. *Shakespeare A to Z: The Essential Reference to His Plays, His Poems, His Life and Times, and More.* Delta; Reissue edition, December 3, 1991.

Boswell-Stone, W. G. *Shakespeare's Holinshed, The Chronicle and The Historical Plays Compared.* Chatto and Windus, Publishers, 1907.

Brooke, Tucker. *Shakespeare of Stratford.* Yale University Press, 1947.

Bryson, Bill. *Shakespeare.* Harper Collins, 2007.

Buckley, Fiona. *The Doublet Affair.* Scribner, 1998.

Burgess, Anthony. *A Dead Man in Deptford.* Carroll & Graf, 1993.

Burgess, Anthony. *Nothing Like the Sun.* W. W. Norton Company, 1964.

Burgess, Anthony. *Shakespeare.* Penguin Books, 1970.

Burton, S. H. *Shakespeare's Life and Stage.* Chambers, 1989.

Cecil, David. *The Cecils of Hatfield House.* Houghton Mifflin, 1973.

Chalfant, Fran C. *Ben Jonson's London: A Jacobean Placename Dictionary.* Univ of Georgia Press, 1978.

Chute, Marchette. *Shakespeare of London.* Dutton; Book Club (BCE/BOMC) edition,1996.

Clark, Sandra. *The Hutchinson Shakespeare Dictionary.* Helicon Publishing, 1993.

Cooper, Susan. *King of Shadows.* Aladdin Paperbacks, 1999.

Cowell, Stephanie. *Nicholas Cooke A Novel.* W. W. Norton, 1993.

Davis, Michael Justin, *The Landscape of William Shakespeare.* Webb and Bower, 1987.

Duncan-Jones, Katherine. *Ungentle Shakespeare.* Thomson Learning, 2001.

Dunton-Downer, Leslie, Alan Riding. *Essential Shakespeare Handbook.* DK Publishing, 2004.

Emerson, Kathy Lynn. *The Writer's Guide to Everyday Life in Renaissance England.* Belgrave House, 2010.

Epstein, Norrie. *The Friendly Shakespeare.* Penguin Books, 1993.

Fraser, Russell. *Young Shakespeare.* Columbia University Press, 1988.

French, Marilyn. *Shakespeare's Division of Experience.* Ballalntine Books, 1981.

Garrett, George. *Entered From The Sun The Murder of Marlowe.* Harcourt Brace Jovanovich, 1990.

George, Margaret. *Mary Queen of Scotland and the Isles.* St. Martin's Press, 1992.

Gielgud, *Acting Shakespeare.* Charles Scribner's Sons, 1991.

Greenblat, Stephen. *Will in the World.* W. W. Norton Company, 2004.

Greer, Germaine. *Shakespeare: A Very Short Introduction.* Oxford University Press, 2002.

Greer, Germaine. *Shakespeare's Wife.* Bloomsbury, 2007.

Gross, Kenneth. *Shylock Is Shakespeare.* University of Chicago Press, 2006.

Harper, Karen. *Mistress Shakespeare.* G. P. Putnam's Sons, 2009.

Harrison, G. B. *Introducing Shakespeare.* Penguin Books, 1966.

Hill, Wayne F. and Ottchen, Cynthia J. *Shakespeare's Insults: Educating Your Wit.* Crown Archetype, 2007.

Hoffman, Calvin. *The Murder of the man who was 'Shakespeare'.* Julian Messer, 1955.

Holden, Anthony. *William Shakespeare The Man Behind the Genius.* William Brown, 1999.

Honan, Park. *Shakespeare A Life.* Oxford University Press, 1998.

Honigman, E. A. J. *Shakespeare: the lost years.* Manchester University Press, 1998.

Hutton, W. H. *Highways and Byways in Shakespeare's Country.* MacMillan, 1914.

Kott, Jan. *Shakespeare our Contemporary.* W. W. Norton, 1966.

Laroque, Francois. *Shakespeare Court, Crowd and Playhouse.* Thames and Hudson, 1991.

Lee, Sidney. *A Life of William Shakespeare.* Oracle Publishing, 1996.

Levi, Peter. *The Life and Times of William Shakespeare.* Henry Holt and Company, 1988.

Macrone, Michael and Lulevitch, Tom. *Brush Up Your Shakespeare.* Harper Paperbacks, 2000.

Macrone, Michael. *Naughty Shakespeare.* Gramercy Books, 1997.

Maxwell, Robin. *The Queen's Bastard.* Arcade Publishing, 1999.

McGregor, Tom. *Elizabeth.* Avon Books, 1988.

Miles, Rosalind. *I, Elizabeth.* Pan Books Ltd, 1994.

Miner, Margaret and Rawson, Hugh. *A Dictionary of Quotations from Shakespeare.* Signet, 1994.

Mortimer, John. *Will Shakespeare An Entertainment.* Hodder and Stoughton, 1977.

O'Connor, Evangeline M. *Who's Who and What's What in Shakespeare.* Gramercy Books, 1978.

O'Connor, Garry. *William Shakespeare A Life.* Sceptre, 1992.

O'Day, Rosemary. *The Tudor Age.* Longman, 1995.

Papp, Joseph and Kirkland, Elizabeth. *Shakespeare Alive!* Bantam Books, 1988.

Picard, Liza. *Elizabeth's London.* Phoenix, 2004.

Pressler, Mirjam. *Shylock's Daughter.* Macmillan Children's Books, 2001.

Price, Merlin. *Folktales and Legends of Warwickshire.* Minimax Books, 1982.

Prockter, Adrian and Taylor, Robert. *The A to Z of Elizabethan London.* Harry Margary, Lympne Castle, Kent, 1979.

Razzell, Peter. *William Shakespeare The Anatomy of an Enigma.* Caliban Books, 1990.

Reynolds, Peter. *Teaching Shakespeare.* Oxford University Press, 1997.

Rosenblum, Joseph. *A Reader's Guide to Shakespeare.* Barnes & Noble Press, 1998.

Rowse, A. L. *The Annotated Shakespeare.* Orbis Publishing, 1978.

Rowse, A. L. *William Shakespeare: A Biography.* Barnes & Noble Books,1995.

Sams, Eric. *The Real Shakespeare: Retrieving the Early Years, 1564-1594.* Yale University Press; Reprint edition, 1997.

Schmidt, Alexander, *Shakespeare Lexicon and Quotation Dictionary.* Dover, 1971.

Schoenbaum, S. *Shakespeare's Lives.* Clarendon Press, 1991.

Schoenbaum, S. *William Shakespeare A Compact Documentary Life.* Oxford University Press, 1987.

Schoenbaum, S. *William Shakespeare A Documentary Life.* Oxford University Press, 1975.

Shapiro, James. *A Year in the Life of William Shakespeare 1599.* Harper Collins, 2005.

Singman, Jeffrey L. *Daily Life in Elizabethan England.* Greenwood Press, 1995.

Spevack, Marvin. *A Shakespeare Thesaurus.* Georg Olms Verlag, 1993.

Sutherland, John and Watts, Cedric. *Henry V, War Criminal?* Oxford University Press, 2000.

Tey, Josephine. *The Daughter of Time.* Scribner Paperback Fiction, 1951.

Thomas, David. *Shakespeare in the Public Records.* Her Majesty's Stationery Office, 1985.

Thomson, Peter. *Shakespeare's Professional Career.* Cambridge University Press, 1999.

Thomson, Peter. *Shakespeare's Theatre.* Routledge, 1992.

Tiffany, Grace. *My Father had a Daughter.* Berkley Books, 2003.

Tiffany, Grace. *Will A Novel.* Berkley Books, 2004.

Updike, John. *Gertrude and Claudius.* Alfred A. Knopf, 2000.

Van Doren, Mark. *Shakespeare.* Doubleday, 1965.

Vendler, Helen. *The Art of Shakespeare's Sonnets.* Harvard University Press, 1997.

Weir, Allison. *The Life of Elizabeth I.* Ballantine Books, 2003.

Wilson, Ian. *Shakespeare: The Evidence.* St. Martin's Griffin, 1999.

Wilson, Jean. *The Shakespeare Legacy.* Bramley Books, 1995.

Yates, F. A. *John Florio- The Life of an Italian in Shakespeare's England.* Cambridge University Press, 1934.

Shakespeare's Family in Succeeding Years

Some people wonder if any direct Shakespeare descendants are alive today, more than four hundred years since Will Shakespeare shuffled off this goodly frame, this earth.

The short answer is NO.

Here's the details about how that occurred:

Will and Anne's children were Susanna and the fraternal twins Hamnet and Judith.

Susanna (1583-1649) married the prosperous Stratford physician John Hall (1575-1635) in 1607. Their only child was Elizabeth (1608-1670). Elizabeth married wealthy barrister Thomas Nash in 1626, and they moved into the Shakespeare home, New Place, also occupied by her grandmother, Anne. Nash died in 1645, leaving no children. In 1649, Elizabeth married again, this time to John Barnard, who was knighted in 1661. They lived in Abington Manor, in Northhamptonshire with Barnard's eight children from a previous marriage. Elizabeth and John Barnard had no children of their own.

The twins Hamnet and Judith had a far worse fate. Hamnet (1585-1596) died of unknown causes at age eleven, so that guaranteed Will and Anne would have no direct descendants bearing the Shakespeare name in the next generation. Judith (1585-1661) survived a good bit longer, but had a rocky time of it. She married a vintner, Thomas Richard Quiney (1589-1662) in 1616. Along with a few legal troubles. they had three children , Shakespeare (Nov 1616-May 1617), Richard (1618-1639) and Thomas (1620-1639). None of the Quiney children produced offspring.

Will's brothers, Gilbert, Richard, and Edmund never married, so that branch of the Shakespeare family name died with Hamnet in 1596.

But, some portion of the Shakespeare DNA did survive. Will's only other sibling that survived to adulthood, his sister Joan (1569-1646), married a local hatter, William Henry Hart (1569-1616). The Harts had several sons who then produced a substantial number of offspring, including Charles Hart (1625-1683). Charles, Will's grandnephew, was an actor. After the English Civil War, there came the Restoration of theatres, and Charles moved to London and began playing women's parts. Eventually, he became well-known for playing Hotspur, the eldest son of the Earl of Northumberland in Will's play Henry IV Part 1. Not only did the Harts reproduce, they added to their family tree by marrying into the families of Wrenn, Page, Linville, Hendricks, Bryan, Richards, Price, Baldwin, Mealis, Buffington, Coburn, Hannum, Gray, Griest, Beals, Underwood, Squibb, and Kilner.

Thus, shirt-tail Shakespeare relatives are undoubtedly among us today, but without the Shakespeare name.

But, if you're interested in who might be today's version of Shakespeare in terms of talent, don't despair that you might have to search the higher realms of academe for his successors. After all, Will was hardly a classic scholar, full of erudition, writing high class literature for erudite scholars. He was a hungry genius who wrote plays that appealed to the tastes of all, especially the common man. So, what recent popular artists might people be reading about in four hundred years when their genres become established in high-brow studies?

Here are some suggestions:

Lin-Manuel Miranda for rap-based plays,
Shonda Rhimes, for TV drama,
Stan Lee, for comic books,
The Notorious B. I. G. for rap music,
Leon Neyfakh's (Slow Burn from Slate) for podcasts,
Katy Perry for tweets.
Or, might something replace reading in four hundred years?

Will's Finances- Income, Expenditures, Accumulation (All Approximate)

Will Shakespeare had several income sources:

1. Salary from an acting troupe- Actors were notoriously poorly-paid. They made anywhere from £12-20/year.
2. Play-writing fees- acting troupes paid anywhere from £10 to £18 for a play, and, if several authors were involved, the money would be split. Second-night privilege grants the author the box office proceeds if a play runs twice in a row, so popular plays can almost double the author's take.
3. Written works, especially poetry, were printed and sold, and some of the proceeds went to the author.
4. Patrons sometimes commissioned works or rewarded authors who dedicated works to them.
5. Acting troupes on tour in the countryside split the proceeds from admissions.
6. Performances for royalty or other private parties earned performance fees.
7. Owners of the troupe split the admissions collected at the box office.
8. Theatre owners collected rent from the troupes, and money from food and drink concessions.
9. Farm owners collected rent and a share of produce sales from tenants.

Will's expenses included:

1. Personal living expenses since he lived in London, away from his family.
2. Family living expenses for those left in Stratford.
3. Purchase of a house (New Place).
4. Renovation of the house.
5. House servants.
6. Investments (Will bought a share in the troupe; held part ownership of The Theatre, the Globe, Blackfriars, and he bought farm land near Stratford.)

7. Payment of debt owed by his father.

Here's a chart summarizing the results of extensive research:

The table is based on estimates from a variety of sources, including plague closings, weather, royal succession, play revenues, living costs, and land transaction records. All entries are in Elizabethan era £. To convert to modern $ requires a multiplier of 300-1000.

Year	Salary	Playwriting	Poetry	Patron	Touring	Royal Perf	Box Office Share	Owners Share	Farm Land	Living Exp	Farm Exp	House Purch	Renovation	House Staff	Investments	Debt Payoff	Net Worth
1590	15									10							0
1591	15	5								10	5						0
1592	18	10	3							12	10						4
1593	4		3	8	3					3	12						4
1594	20	20	4	25		4	20			10	12				20		35
1595	20	60	4		5	8	25			10	15						132
1596	20	60	4		5	10	15			12	15	60					149
1597	20	60	5			10	10			12	20						167
1598	10	60	3			15	12	40		13	25		30	20	30		169
1599		50	3			15	80	50		12	25			40			252
1600		50	3			15	90	50		15	25			45			365
1601		45				14	90	50	40	16	25			45		88	391
1602		35				30	20	20	40	16	25			45	320		174
1603		30				30	90	50	40	16	25			45			228
1604		30				20	90	50	90	16	25			45			382
1605		25				20	80	40	90	16	25			45	440		521
1606		25				20	80	40	90	16	25			45			250
1607		25				20	110	60	90	16	25			45	100		419
1608		30				20	120	60	90	16	25			45			543
1609		30				30	120	60	90		25			45			777
1610		25					120	60	90		25			45			1016
1611							100	20	90		25			45			1196
1612							100		90		25			45			1370
1613							50		90		25			45			1466
1614									90		25			45			1486
1615									90		25			45			1506

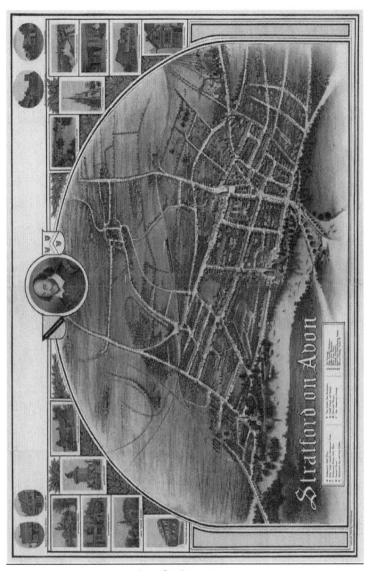

Stratford on Avon

Brown, J. Ross. *Stratford on Avon*. [England?: J. Ross Brown, 1908] Map.
https://www.loc.gov/item/93686544/.

197

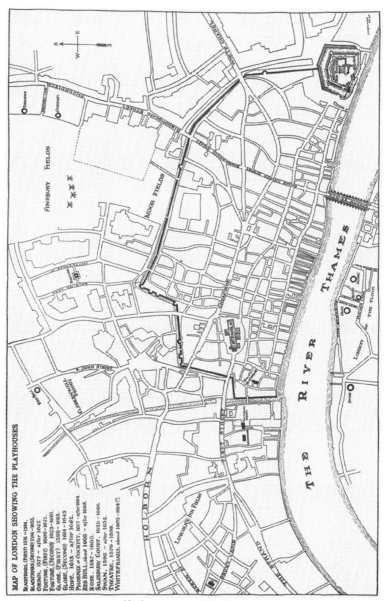

Shakespearean Playhouses

The Project Gutenberg eBook, Shakespearean Playhouses, by Joseph Quincy Adams, Image credit C. W. Redwood, formerly technical artist at Cornell University

About the Authors

This book has been a labor of love for us, since we have had a Shakespeare hobby/obsession for almost thirty years. To this end, we have:

- ✓ traveled to England several times,
- ✓ followed Shakespeare's route from Stratford to London on bicycles,
- ✓ saw every play either live or on video, multiple times,
- ✓ visited several Shakespearean venues in various states and countries,
- ✓ become a Friend of the New Globe in London and watched it built,
- ✓ visited the Folger Shakespeare Library in Washington,
- ✓ read 100+ books about Shakespeare's life, the plays, and Elizabethan times,
- ✓ visited countless websites dealing with Shakespearean topics.

Both of us are retired educators, and we are experienced writers and editors, but our specialty has been non-fiction. So our novelistic efforts have been critiqued by several independent editors over many years. These editors have helped enormously, most recently Sharon Schumer Schwartz.

Besides the fabulous cover caricature by our friend Sidney Harris, we have greatly appreciated not only our tireless literary agent, Nancy Rosenfeld, but also agents of inspiration along the way, notably Al Varone, Paul Winston, Gerry Faye, Allen Galin, and most significantly, Carol DeVore. Thanks loads for all your help.

Arthur W. Wiggins and Barbara M. Wiggins

Full Disclosure: William Cecil, Queen Elizabeth's Secretary of State for much of her reign is Art Wiggins' 11th great grandfather.

Made in the USA
Middletown, DE
20 August 2019